PERSONALIZED STRESS MANAGEMENT

A Manual for Everyday Life and Work

Joseph L. Gill M.S.

Counseling & Consulting Services Publications

Counseling & Consulting Services
4020 Moorpark Avenue • Suite 204
San Jose, CA 95117 • (408) 246-1128

Published by:

Counseling & Consulting Services Publications
     Counseling & Consulting Services
     4020 Moorpark Avenue, Suite 204
     San Jose, California 95117
     (408) 246-1128

Library of Congress Cataloging in Publication Data
     Gill, Joseph L., 1939-
        Personalized stress management.

        Bibliography: p.
        1. Stress (Psychology)--Prevention--Problems,
        exercises, etc. I. Title.
     BF575.S75G54 1983   158'.1   82-90115
     ISBN 0-910819-00-9
     ISBN 0-910819-01-7 (pbk.)

DEDICATION

To my mother and father:

Helen and Luther Gill

ACKNOWLEDGEMENTS

My first acknowledgement is attributed to my niece, Henrietta Wallace, who completed the typesetting and composition layout for this book. Her tolerance, occasional criticisms, and intricate comments were especially helpful.

A special thank you goes to the following people: Rain Blockley for her excellence in the editing of the original manuscript, and Diane Lawrence for the typing; Steve Naegele for the design of the book cover and photography of the illustrations of exercises for stress indicators, and Darline Michol for modeling the exercises; and all others who have read, commented, edited, transcribed, or typed portions of the manuscript, Frank Ciena, Eunice Wallace, Roberto De Villar, Linda Leonard, and Susan Mandell to name a few.

Further appreciation is extended to Hugh Schade, M.D., James Higgins, D.D.S., and Leo Stuart, M. D. for their review and critique of the final manuscript draft.

Finally, I wish to express gratitude to my entire family, all my friends and loved ones, associates, clients, and students who have all been very much a part of my personal life and professional experiences, that have attributed to my confidence and competence in the overall completion of this work.

Joseph Gill

CONTENTS

PART I UNDERSTANDING STRESS

PART II STRESS COPING METHODS

PART III STRESS MANAGEMENT PROGRAM

PREFACE

Stress is a natural, unavoidable, and often, necessary reaction. It is a perfectly normal response to everyday challenges of life and work. However, when stress is accrued beyond one's level of tolerance and skills of self-management, the reactions become unnatural, abnormal, and often, irrational. These responses can have critical effects on the individual's mental and physical functioning.

When people become stressed beyond their level of self-help and personal control they may seek the assistance of a professional that specializes in the area of difficulty they are suffering. If the stress has a physiological base or causes physical impairment or discomfort, they usually consult a physician. If the stress is psychological in nature and causes mental or physical dysfunction that do not require medication, ordinarily the services of a mental health professional are solicited.

In my experience as a therapist, in treating persons (when undergoing treatment, referred to as patients) who suffer from stress difficulties and related illnesses, it has become apparent that in each case, the prognosis (chances of cure) is very much dependent on the patient's potential to be his own therapist; and that this potential must be actualized in order for cure to take place.

Generally speaking, when people seek therapy, it is for one of two reasons: either they feel too overwhelmed and powerless to take responsibility for making changes necessary to alleviate their stress (or make satisfactory adjustments for coping), or, they lack the skills to do so. In more extreme cases one can often suffer from both. In therapy what constitutes the patient's cure (response to treatment) is his ability to gain a sense of power and take responsibility. Therapy is terminated when the patient is either in control of the event or situation that is causing stress, or has made necessary changes for alleviation and/or satisfactory adjustments.

Therapy, in a clinical sense is merely a combination of theory(s), skills, approaches, and methods of application in relation to a particular disorder, illness, or discomfort. The professional, having an understanding of the theory(s), mastered the skills of application, and practiced them on his patients is called a therapist.

A person undergoing treatment from his therapist, if asked, "What are you receiving for your illness?", he would reply no doubt, "Therapy". If asked, "What is therapy?", his most logical answer in all consideration would be his therapist's understanding of theory, and skills of application, in relation to the illness he suffers.

As the therapist renders therapy, more so than providing a cure he is offering the patient the essentials for cure that will bring about relief when and if the patient makes use of them.

The therapist can offer limited aspects of theory, teach skills of application and provide guidance, offer support for the patient's efforts of application and give reinforcement to accomplishments, but the application of understanding, knowledge and skill related to the difficulty must be carried out by the patient. In this sense, the patient is curing himself.

To expand, it seems that much of what the patient learns in therapy he could learn on his own, and if practiced often enough, could be mastered. Whereby, if and when a similar difficulty is incurred, to a great extent, he would be able to cure himself, or at least take or develop preventive measures that would minimize his need for professional help.

It is not always the fault of the general public (often referred to as the layman) that they do not have the understanding and skills that would help prevent or eliminate the difficulties that cause stress. For the most part, books that are written on the subject of stress (or related problems, disorders, illnesess, etc.) are written by professionals for professionals to teach their students who are going to become professionals. The author(s) either over-analyze or belabor their thesis to the point that after a few chapters the reader begins to wonder why he is trying to complete the book, or the readability of the material presented is often beyond the laymen's comprehension. Unless the technical language and scientific jargon is interpreted by a professional in the field, the general public who could benefit most from the content of the book, is kept mystified or at the mercy of the professional to help him understand and make use of the information.

In the writing and production of **Personalized Stress Management (PSM)**, I have made every effort to avoid these pitfalls. **PSM** contains an abundance of general information, on a wealth of prevalent stress-related topics, that much of the concerned public does not know how to make use of or does not have. To maintain the readers's interest, the information presented is organized, well paced, concise, and wherever possible, written in the first person to secure a more personal writer-to-reader communication. To certify lay understanding and readability, for the initial editing, editors who were not necessarily professionally sophisticated on the topic of stress were chosen. Only after the original draft of the book was completed, was it re-edited and reviewed for technical accuracy by medical authorities in the field.

PSM is designed to help the reader develop self-reliance and confidence that will place his inner self as the locus of control over how he is affected by external forces, events, and situations that are stressful. Its conceptual meaning implies (1) an understanding of stress, (2) the ability to identify stressors and their source, (3) a sufficient and adequate repertoire of skills and methods of approach that can be directly applied to stress reduction, coping, alleviation, or satisfactory adjustment, and (4) an ongoing preventive stress management program that keeps stress at a minimum.

People who do not have **Personalized Stress Management** do not recognize their own responsibility in their condition of stress and how they are affected. They see the control of stress as other directed and beyond their own self-regulation. When they become physically or mentally ill as a result of too much stress, they do not think of what they can do for themselves, but more so of what a physician or therapist can do. Often they just "sit" on the problem that causes them stress and hope it goes away on its own. Just before a breaking point (i.e., becoming completely dysfunctional) they rush out to seek professional help and expect a "crash cure" (immediate crisis resolution).

When individuals or couples consult me for private counseling, what is first and primary on their minds is, "What can he do to help me relieve my stress?". However, as I listen to them reveal the cause and nature of their difficulties, what goes through my mind is, "What can I do to help them help themselves?". And, this is the manner in which I proceed with treatment. The process begins by:

Reflective listening and history-taking for a broad prospective of the problem and its relevant precipitants, an analysis and inter-pretation of the difficulty to establish an operational definition, and an assessment of the various approaches and resources available to the client that will help relieve his stress. The client's potential for making use of available resources is also evaluated.

When this is completed, the steps that follow are: assessment of the strength of the difficulty, setting goals for resolution of the problem, mapping a plan of approach to achieve these goals, making a commitment to follow through with the plan, and finally, periodic evaluations of the plan. This pro-cess is continued or repeated until the problem is resolved, or all avenues of reso-lution are exhausted.

Essentially this procedure is a **PSM** developmental process and as much as possible, has been incorporated into the overall format of the book.

Personalized Stress Management is designed to help those who do not have a sense of personal control and mastery over stress in their life. For those who do, **PSM** provides an opportunity to expand their supply of skills, increases competence, and enhances self-confidence needed for continued progress in keeping stress at a self-management level. These elements foster more natural reactions to the demands and pressures of daily living, and assure better mental and physical health.

Joseph L. Gill

Part I.

UNDERSTANDING STRESS

CHAPTER 1.

About Stress

WHAT IS STRESS ?

Several connotative words are frequently used to describe stress or feelings of stress, including tension, anxiety, frustration, strain, and pressure. All of these words constitute some mental or physical effect on the body. By the time these words come into play, stress is generally at a state in which there is a demand or urgency for action that will generate relief. When this state occurs we must adapt, cope, or adjust. Stress prior to this point, in general, does nothing to disturb or disrupt the existing equilibrium of the mind or the body. From this premise, stress will be defined as: anything or any situation that disrupts or disturbs the existing equilibrium of our mind and body, gradually or abruptly, in such a way that it demands adaptation, coping, or adjusting.

Inherent in this definition of stress is that our body, when under stress changes from a state of relative calm to a state of excitation. This change is in response and reaction to changes in our environment and could be real or imagined, pleasant or unpleasant.

STRESS AND CHANGE

As a result of their research into the extent of stress produced by change, social psychologists Holmes and Rahe (9) constructed a scale of stress values called the **Life Change Scale**. After assigning an arbitrary baseline value of fifty Life Change Units (LCUs) to the act of marriage, they asked people of various national, racial, ethnic, and socio-economic backgrounds to rate the stress produced by other actions and events. The most stressful event on the scale turned out to be death of a spouse and was given the value of 100 LCUs. By comparison, minor violations of the law were given 11 LCUs. The object of the research was to show the correlation between the stress of life's changes (and/or critical changes in an individual's experiences) and the effort required to adapt, cope, or adjust. The researchers also felt that stressful events reduce the body's natural defenses against disease and illness and increase the tendency to be accident-prone.
==

REFLECTION

The **Life Change Scale** may be used to determine how much stress you are subjecting yourself to as a result of changes in your life. To use the scale, simply record the value amounts of the LCUs for all the life events you have experienced during the last twelve months (in the brackets provided under your LCUs). Add up your total LCU score and compare the totals to the standards listed below:

         0 to 150:   No significant problems

         150 to 199:   Mild crisis
                          (33% chance of illness)

         200 to 299:   Moderate life crisis
                          (50% chance of illness)

         300 or over: Major life crisis
                          (80% chance of illness)

LIFE CHANGE SCALE

Rank	Life Event	Life Crisis Units (LCUs)	Your LCUs
1.	Death of a Spouse	100	( )
2.	Divorce	73	( )
3.	Marital Separation	65	( )
4.	Jail Term	63	( )
5.	Death of a close family member	63	( )
6.	Personal injury or illness	53	( )
7.	Marriage	50	( )
8.	Fired at work	47	( )
9.	Marital reconciliation	45	( )
10.	Retirement	45	( )
11.	Change in health of family member	44	( )
12.	Pregnancy	40	( )
13.	Sex difficulties	39	( )
14.	Gain of new family member	39	( )
15.	Business readjustment	38	( )
16.	Change in financial state	38	( )
17.	Death of a close friend	37	( )
18.	Change to a different line of work	36	( )
19.	Change in number of arguments with spouse	35	( )
20.	Mortgage over $10,000	31	( )
21.	Foreclosure of mortgage or loan	30	( )
22.	Change in responsibilities at work	29	( )
23.	Son or daughter leaving home	29	( )
24.	Trouble with in-laws	29	( )
25.	Outstanding personal achievement	28	( )
26.	Wife begins or stops work	26	( )
27.	Begin or end school	26	( )
28.	Change in living conditions -	25	( )
29.	Revision of personal habits	24	( )
30.	Trouble with boss	23	( )
31.	Change in work hours or conditions	20	( )
32.	Change in residence	20	( )
33.	Change in school	20	( )
34.	Change in recreation	19	( )
35.	Change in church activities	19	( )
36.	Change in social activities	18	( )
37.	Mortgage or loan less than $10,000	17	( )
38.	Change in sleeping habits	16	( )

39.	Change in number of family get-togethers	15	( )
40.	Change in eating habits	15	( )
41.	Vacation	13	( )
42.	Christmas	12	( )
43.	Minor violations of the law	11	( )
	Your total LCU:		( )

Source: Holmes and Rahe, "The Social Readjustment Rating Scale," Journal of Psychosomatic Research, 1967. By permission
==

Although this scale is correlational rather than a factual finding, there is little doubt that it can serve as a useful indicator of your predisposition for disease and illness due to stress caused by significant life changes. That is, when your score exceeds 300 LCUs in twelve months, chances are that you are in a major life crisis and are more vulnerable to illness than someone who has scored a lower rate. When this is so, you should avoid additional stress and make compensations to lower the amount of stress in your life as much as possible. This can often be done by making adjustments in your lifestyle and activities, and minimizing new responsibilities.

As you can see from the **Life Change Scale,** not all stress is unpleasant. Foreclosure on a mortgage loan can be just as stressful as buying a new home, and filing bankruptcy can be just as stressful as winning a state lottery, though the latter in each case is preferred. Stress is anything that frustrates us, thrills us, worries us, excites us, or depresses us. In fact, when we speak of life it would be difficult to think of anything that is not stressful. It is all a matter of degree.

KINDS OF STRESS

There are basically two kinds of stress: emotional (mental) and physical, both of which can be either desired and healthy or undesired and unhealthy. As with the coordination and interaction of the mind and body, emotional stress can lead to physical stress and physical stress can lead to emotional stress. Accordingly, we find that there are dual sources of both mental and physical stress. These dual sources come into play, for example, when we are under mental pressure to get a physical job done and under physical pressure to get a mental job done.

Physical stress occurs when we use physical strength or muscular force for movement and activities,e.g., lifting, pulling, walking, playing a sport, or doing daily and routine chores. Mental stress takes place during cognitive processing, e.g., thinking, planning, and administrative activities. Jobs and professions requiring essentially physical activities are usually skilled, semi-skilled, or unskilled clerical and labor work. Those requiring, for the most part, mental and emotional stress are professional, paraprofessional, administrative, and managerial positions. In either case, whether the work calls for predominantly physical or mental stress, a job that becomes overly demanding and monotonous can lead to physical as well as mental and emotional stress.

To a certain extent, stress is necessary for normal functioning. It appears that a mild level of arousal is necessary to produce alertness and interest in whatever task is at hand. As most of us know from experience, boredom itself can be stressful. When life is too quiet and peaceful for too long, we develop a drive for excitement, e.g., so we go to a horror or science fiction movie, find an interesting book to read, engage in sports or exercise, or do something to stimulate ourselves.

Our nervous system apparently needs a certain

amount of stress and stimulation to function properly and effectively. Many of us just cannot seem to get going unless we are under some kind of stress. When we are not under stress, we tend to procrastinate and become lackadaisical about getting the job done. The stress that is inherent in all new challenges of life is warranted and healthy; it becomes unwarranted and unhealthy only when it reaches a level of intensity or is prolonged to the extent that it has destructive physical or psychological effects.

We all react in different ways to unhealthy physical and psychological stress. Under severe and prolonged stress, some people develop pathological mental conditions that lead to neurosis, psychosis, various forms of character disorders, or dependencies. Other people develop physical disorders. Common physical disorders associated with prolonged and severe stress range from headaches, back pain, and muscular tensions to more serious diseases of hives, asthma, hypertension, ulcers, and colitis.

These diseases are often identified as diseases of adaptation. Unlike their primitive ancestors, modern men and women are unable to make use of the inherited fight-or-flight reactions that are aroused in dangerous and threatening situations. Adaptation to modern life requires that we suppress our fight reaction and adjust our reaction to flee. We are required to inhibit our natural expressions and emotions and, accordingly, we induce an intense and often prolonged state of unresolved conflict that takes a destructive toll on our bodies.

ROOTS OF STRESS:

The roots of stress are found in frustration and conflict. These states are generaly interrelated. Frustration quite often ends in conflict; and in our efforts to resolve the conflict, we are often frustrated further. For example, consider a high school graduate who asks a girl to his senior prom and is refused. He is frustrated when his goal and desire is thwarted by the girl's refusal, and deciding how he should or will respond to that refusal could lead to conflict. Should he ask her again at another time, give up on her and risk asking another girl, or change his plans and cancel going to the prom?

Choosing a course of action entails confronting these conflicting options. The interrelation of frustration and conflict continues even after a course of action is selected. If the student asks the same girl again, she may refuse him again. If he asks another girl, she may also refuse. If he cancels his plans to go to the prom, he runs the risk of embarrassment, or it may be too late to get a refund on the tickets he paid for in advance. Thus, his attempts to resolve his frustration and conflict may produce new frustrations.

Frustration can be described as an emotional state of stress that results when an obstacle or barrier prevents the achievement of a goal or the satisfaction of desires, needs, or expectations. The variety of obstacles and barriers that cause frustration are infinite. They range from simple physical obstructions and interference to more complex personal inadequacies. Trying to get to work on time but suddenly running into a traffic jam, trying to buy a new home but being unable to qualify for a loan, and failing a graduate records exam after extended efforts of study, are but a few examples.

Conflict is described as a condition of stress that is produced when one has two or more incompatible or opposing courses of action that can be taken to meet one's desires, needs, or expectations. An individual in conflict feels pulled in different directions at the same time.

Conflicts are classified according to whether the individual is attracted to or repelled by the available courses of action. In general, there are

three such classifications: approach-approach,
avoidance-avoidance, and approach-avoidance.

In **approach-approach** conflicts, stress results from
a situation wherein individuals have to choose
between two or more equally attractive (positive)
goals, wants, or desires. A classic example of
this type of conflict is the donkey that starved to
death between two bales of hay. As the story
relates, the donkey couldn't decide which bale to
approach because they both looked delicious. We
encounter similar approach-approach conflicts in
our everyday lives: we go to the store and have
trouble choosing between two or more name brands of
merchandise, we have difficulty deciding between
the style or color of two pairs of shoes. Of the
three types of conflicts, approach-approach choices
are the most easily resolved because either choice
will be acceptable. A conflict arises only because
the options are equally desirable and mutually
exclusive; and for many people, because "the grass
always looks greener on the other side of the
fence", they have difficulty making decisions under
such conditions.

In **avoidance-avoidance** conflicts, stress results
from situations wherein individuals have to choose
between two or more equally repulsive (negative)
alternatives. For instance, a person is trapped on
the 35th floor of a burning hotel, the only escape
is out the window, and the choices are to jump or
stay and take a chance on burning to death. A
student who has not studied for an exam can either
take the test and risk flunking, or skip the exam
and accept the consequences. A child who has
broken a window while his mother is away at work
can either call her and let her know about the
accident or wait until she comes home and finds out
for herself. Individuals in these situations would
rather avoid both courses of action.

The stress resulting from **approach-avoidance**
conflicts involves individuals who have to choose
between goals, wants, or desires that are

attractive in one way and repulsive in another. This type of conflict is apparent when people use the phrase "yes, but" when making choices and decisions. A woman may like a man's looks and physical appearance, but despise his personality. She may want to get married and raise a family, but at the same time find that she wants to pursue a full-time career. A teenager may want very badly to leave home and get out on his own, but find himself unable to financially support himself. A child may want to pet a nice looking dog, but is afraid it will bite. A man trying to loose weight, goes to a party and finds himself faced with several desserts he has always liked. People caught in approach-avoidance situations are often accused of wanting to have their cake and eat it too. Approach-avoidance conflicts are probably the most confusing and frequently occurring of the three types of conflicts.

Stress is a product of frustration and conflict. Frustration and conflict activate the anxiety and emotional arousal that causes stress. This arousal motivates us to respond to the frustration and conflict that causes us stress. Theoretically speaking, the level of arousal is proportional to the level of frustration and complexity of the conflict. However, as we will see in the chapters that follow, this is seldom the case in real life. Our level of anxiety and emotional arousal in relation to frustration and conflict is basically dependent on our perceptions. Our perceptions are very much dependent on our personality. How we perceive events and situations is partially innate, partially learned, and different for each individual. It is for this reason that stress management through the course of this book is treated as a personalized matter.

CHAPTER 2.

Physiological & Psychological Properties of Stress

ANATOMY OF STRESS

Beginning with our perceptions, stress can result from both internal and external sources. **Internal** sources of stress are mental perceptions produced by our imaginations and reflections of current or past stimuli (situations) perceived as frustrating, conflicting, or emotionally arousing. Stress of this nature is secondary, and because the situation produced is simply imaginary, or if real, adjustments to the original impact has already been made, it elicits minimal excitations.

External sources of stress result from information gathered about situations through our physical senses (vision, hearing, touch, taste, and smell). When the information is received, it goes to the association centers of the brain. There, the incoming information is compared and associated with already existing, or pre-recorded material that is based on previous experiences and perceptions. These comparisons and associations provide mental perceptions that define the external situations in a way that determines how we will be affected. Accordingly, emotions are aroused.

When an external situation is perceived as threatening or dangerous, associations made in the

brain usually trigger such emotions as anger and
fear. These emotions then send out an alarm that
activates our sympathetic nervous system, which in
turn stimulates our adrenal gland. Our bodies are
placed in a full state of alarm both chemically and
electrically. At this point we are fully prepared
for fight or flight. In simultaneous response, the
heart speeds up and pumps more blood to the brain,
muscles, and surface of the skin; the lungs expand
and we breathe harder and faster; the blood sugar
level is elevated; eyes dilate to let in more
light; and digestion is slowed down.

For animals and ancient man, this state of alarm
was the end of the sequence of events in
preparation for dealing with the situation at hand.
The organism would then either fight or flee. When
the threatening situation subsided, the
parasympathetic nervous system would dominate the
sympathetic nervous system and the organism would
return to normal, restoring and rebuilding the
resources that were depleted by the incident. For
modern and socialized man, however, this is not the
case. First, we are seldom faced with situations
that can be solved simply by fighting or fleeing;
and second, we are socialized to suppress
aggression and taught that it is cowardly to flee.
This conditioning places us in conflict with our
instincts, thereby adding stress to the already
existing stress of the situation itself.

So the sequence of reactions triggered by stress is
taken further in modern men and women. While our
bodies are preparing for the fight or flight
reaction, the limbic system, a relatively recent
evolutionary development of man's brain, comes into
play. The limbic system controls our emotional
energy and regulates our reflective behavior while
the brain makes further associations in attempts to
decide how to respond to the situation in a
"socially appropriate way." Most often the
socially appropriate reaction calls more for
adapting, coping, or adjusting to the situation
more so than acting directly in the manner that our

bodies are prepared for. If we are unable to adapt, cope, or adjust in a way that relieves our fight or flight preparation, we suffer physical and mental exhaustion due to the depletion of energy caused by our constant and prolonged state of alarm and conflict. Mental and physical exhaustion results in severe and dysfunctional mental and physical disorders and can even lead to death.

Our ability to adapt, cope, or adjust provides us with resistance to the stressful situation, but does not always completely deactivate the source of stress. Often stressful situations are ongoing and become progressively intense. The pressures of modern and socialized living (such as climbing the corporate ladder, inflated mortgage payments, rising food and fuel prices, recession, and job lay-offs) keep us in a state of alarm for hours, days, months, and even years at a time. Our resistance burns out gradually and often below our level of consciousness. We reach exhaustion an organ at a time. It is most frightening when these organs are our most vital ones.

LEARNED HABITS: COPING WITH STRESS

As children, we come into the world totally egocentric. We have no concern or awareness of the needs of others. Essentially, we have the philosophy of, "I want what I want when I want it." Replies such as, "Wait just a minute," or "I'm just too tired," or "too sleepy," are meaningless to us in our early months of life. During this time, our needs center for the most part around feelings, diaper changes, stroking, and other forms of nurturance.

Our egocentric nature is generally accepted by our parents, who respond on demand to our every beck and call. However, as a matter of socialization, we have to learn at some point that we can't always have our way when we want it, and that the world does not revolve around us.

As a child, stress begins when we receive our first serious "no-no" from our parents. The frustrating remarks of "have to wait," "no-no." "can't have," and the tone of voice in which they are spoken by the parent(s) often produces anxiety in the child and lets him or her know that serious consequences will follow if the remarks are not honored. This frustration and anxiety places the child under stress, and the child or the child's body must in some way respond to this stress. Though the child may not understand the rationale behind the denials and conditional responses given to his demands or requests, or may lack the cognitive maturity to be able to understand, he has to obey and concede to the authority of the parent. When the child obeys or concedes against its will, he is undergoing stress and must learn to adjust. Learning to adjust to, and cope with, stressful situations in life is a natural part of the socialization process for the child.

Through trial and error, imitation, modeling, and teaching, the child learns to respond to stress and stressful situations in a way that is socially acceptable and in consideration of others in his environment. The parents are the primary examples and the authority that provides a framework for the development of the child's character and mode of responding to stress. Their reaction to the stress responses made by the child provide guidance and reinforcement to those responses. According to the parent's reactions, the child will either make the same response again, modify the response, not make the response again, or develop a new response.

Whenever a response to stress is given by the child, and that same response is repeated over a period of time, a habit is formed. This is a learned habit that becomes an integral part of the child's personality for responding to a particular situation of stress and is usually generalized to similar situations. To give an example, suppose a child asks for a glass of milk in a demanding way, such as, "I want my milk." and the parent reacts

with the reply of, "Not until you say please." If
the child responds by throwing a tantrum and the
parent gives in, this would reinforce the child to
throw a tantrum the next time his request is not
met. However, if the parent insists that the child
say "please" and the child is forced or decides to
meet this accommodating condition, this will
reinforce the child to accompany other requests
with the word please.

In other situations, the parents may not offer
accommodating conditions for the child. When a
mother says, "No, you cannot play with my
cosmetics," the child must make some kind of
adjustment in response to its forced suppression of
desire and accompanying emotions. And again, the
parent's reaction to the child's responses will
determine whether the child repeats the response in
similar situations. Many parents favor withdrawal
responses from the child. Other parents help the
child find alternatives, such as pointing out a toy
or something more appropriate for the child to
play with. Still others foster tantrum responses
from the child with various signs of covert
approval such as teasing or smiling. Whichever the
parents reaction, a learning process is taking
place in the child's personality and character
insofar as how it will manage and cope with stress.

The difficulty with learned habits of responding to
stress is that, positive or negative ways of
responding that were learned in childhood and
worked to our advantage then, often tend to work to
our disadvantage as adults. That is, we become
fixated in habits developed in childhood and seldom
assess, reassess, or modify them to meet the
demands that are placed on us as adults. Perhaps
as children we learned to suppress our emotions in
response to stress because we had authoritarian
parents who did not allow emotional outlet, or we
were punished for talking back. As adults,
however, we have more control over our environment
and we have much more freedom to assert our
emotions. If we stick to learned habits of

suppressing our feelings, we subject ourselves to continued and chronic stress.

INTERNALIZERS AND EXTERNALIZERS

Julian Rotter (16) described people as internalizers and externalizers in terms of how they handled stress. Internalizers are people who believe that they are autonomous and masters of their own fate. They tend to take personal responsibility for what happens to them and to see the control of their lives as coming from inside themselves. In doing so, they appeal more to their own intra-psychic resources for dealing with stressful situations. People who are internalizers tend to externalize their problems only when they have exhausted all possible internal resources.

On the other hand, externalizers are seen as people who believe they have little or no control as to what happens to them in their lives. They feel that what happens to them is a matter of good or bad luck, or simply "God's will." They feel that their lives are controlled by forces beyond their control and that they themselves have little or no influence. Externalizers, for the most part, feel that whatever happens to them in all aspects of their lives is a matter of fate. They landed their job or position by luck. If they lose their job or position, it is the "breaks". If they have to commute fifty miles per day in bumper-to-bumper traffic and this has gone on for five years, it is unfortunate. They feel stuck in undesirable and stressful situations no matter what the duration or how stressful the situation is. They seem to wait it out or to feel that "it" will get better with time. More often than not, they feel that the situation will take care of itself so they "sit on it." The trouble with this is that the longer they wait, the more stuck they become. In the process they become numb, soon losing their awareness that they are stuck. More often than not, they also fail to realize that while they are sitting on the

problem, prolonged and undue stress is taking its
toll on their mental and physical health.
===

REFLECTION

What are you, an internalizer or externalizer?

Below are ten pairs of statements constructed by
Julian Rotter. After reading each pair, place a
checkmark in the brackets provided below the
statement that seems most accurate to you.

I more strongly believe that: Or:

(1)

Promotions are earned   Making a lot of
through hard work and   money is largely a
persistence.   matter of getting
                               the right breaks.

    (   )   (   )

(2)

In my experience I have   Many times the
noticed that there   reactions of teach-
is usually a direct   ers seem haphazard
connection between how hard   to me.
I study and the grades I get.

    (   )   (   )

(3)

The number of divorces   Marriage is largely
indicates that more and more   a gamble.
people are not trying to make
their marriages work.

    (   )   (   )

(4)

When I am right I can
convince others.

( )

It is silly to think
one can really change
another person's
basic attitudes.

( )

(5)

In our society, a man's
future earning power is
dependent upon his ability.

( )

Getting promoted is
really a matter of
being luckier than
the next guy.

( )

(6)

If one knows how to deal
with people they are really
quite easily led.

( )

I have little influ-
ence over the way
other people behave.

( )

(7)

In my case the grades I
make are the results of
my own efforts; luck
has little or nothing to
do with it.

( )

Sometimes I feel that
I have little to do
with the grades I
get.

( )

(8)

People like me can change the course of world affairs if we make ourselves heard.	It is only wishful thinking to believe that one can really influence what happens in society at large.
( )	( )

(9)

I am the master of my fate.	A great deal that happens to me is probably a matter of chance.
( )	( )

(10)

Getting along with people is a skill that must be practiced.	It is almost impossible to figure out how to please some people.
( )	( )

Choices on the left indicate a belief in internal control, and choices on the right, external control. Do you have more checks on the left or on the right? Although there are no standards established for this test, a comparison of your totals could be indicative of whether you see internal or external forces as the reasons for what happens to you in life.

Source: Reprinted with the permission of Psychology Today, 1971, Ziff-Davis Publishing Company. New York, NY.
==

In completing the questionnaire, it should be remembered that personalities are not so simple as to fit neatly into such abstract categories as externalizers and internalizers. For the most part, everyone probably has mixed tendencies. Even the most impotent externalizer will in some situations meet stress actively, rather than rationalizing or denying that they exist. And, conversely not always do the most faithful internalizers meet stressful problems head on. However, it can safely be said that people who have high scores as externalizers have stronger tendencies to feel less in control of stressful situations; the reverse is so for persons who score high as internalizers.

BEHAVIORS AND STRESS

In their book Type A Behavior and the Heart (7), cardiologists Friedman and Rosenman categorized people's behavior according to their personality. They described two types of personalities associated with behavior, **Type A** and **Type B**. They felt that these behavior types were better predictors of heart disease than smoking, lack of exercise, poor diet, or overeating. They described Type A persons as highly competitive, ambitious, and impatient. They eat fast, walk briskly, and rush others. The Type A persons are list makers. They try to eat, shave, and listen to or read the news all at the same time. They feel guilty relaxing, are seldom satisfied, and demand continual self-improvement.

Type B persons are described as persons not plagued by Type A behaviors. Type B persons are more relaxed, less ambitious, and more patient; they have fewer irons in the fire and pace themselves rather than hurrying and scurrying around. They focus more on the quality of life, smoke less, and have fewer heart attacks.
==

REFLECTIONS

Do you have more Type A or Type B characteristics?
To find out, answer yes or no to the questions
below. **Yes** answers are characteristic of Type A
persons and **No** answers are characteristic of Type
B.

DO YOU:

(   ) 1.   Have a habit of strongly accentuating
various key words in your day to day
speech even when there is no real
need.

(   ) 2.   Always move, walk, and eat at a rapid
pace.

(   ) 3.   Feel impatient with the rate that
most events seem to take place.

(   ) 4.   Feel an urge or make attempts to
finish sentences of persons speaking
to you before they can.

(   ) 5.   Find it upsetting to watch others
perform routine tasks, e.g. writing
checks, filling out forms, reading
directions, etc.

(   ) 6.   Become highly upset and irritated
when obliged to perform routine
tasks, e.g., writing checks, filling
out forms, reading directions, etc.

(   ) 7.   Find it terribly annoying to be
stuck in slow moving traffic or
having to wait in line to be seated
in a restaurant.

(   ) 8.   Always find yourself trying to find
condensations that will summarize
what you are reading to hurry you
through an article or book even when

it is interesting and worthwhile.

(   ) 9.   Consistently try to do more than one thing at the same time, e.g., eat, shave, and read the morning paper, or listen to a person talk about one thing and you ponder another that you think is more important.

(   ) 10. Feel guilty when you relax or take time out to do nothing.

(   ) 11. Always attempt to bring the theme of a conversation you are involved in around to topics of your particular interest and proficiency.

(   ) 12. Attempt to crowd more and more things to do in less and less time with little regards for unexpected contingencies.

(   ) 13. Dedicate all your time to things worth having to the extent you have no time for things worth being.

(   ) 14. Find yourself competitive with other Type A persons.

Source: Adapted from Type A Behavior and your Heart, by Meyer Friedman, M. D. and Ray H. Rosenman, M. D., by permission of Alfred A. Knopf, Inc. Copyright 1974 by Meyer Friedman.

===

Though the findings by Friedman and Rosenman that Type A persons are more prone to heart related diseases is correlational rather than factual, their followup studies have shown consistently that Type A persons develop illnesses and diseases at twice the rate of Type B persons.

Type A Behavior in and of itself is not harmful and

can be seen as a positive trait. Type A persons
certainly are more practical and tend to get more
things done and in shorter periods of time than
Type B persons. However, it is the Type A person
that loses sight of their energy level and the
body's signal for needs of rest and rejuvenation
that create health problems due to over-exertion.
Without this awareness, Type A persons tend to slow
down only when their bodies demand it through
burnout and illness. Their adrenalin is high
because of their excitement and pressure to reach
their goals. They lose consciousness of their
diminishing energy supply and reserve, and
declining resistance, which makes them more prone
to heart-related diseases and medical difficulties.

The character of a Type A person runs on a
continuum from moderate to extreme. Those at the
extreme are at a constant state of tension and tend
to push and drive themselves beyond their physical
capacity. If you feel you are at this extreme end
of the Type A person continuum, you might give some
serious consideration to making personal
commitments to minimize or modify your behavior.
Later chapters in this book offer means of
combating and balancing Type A behavior through
developing an awareness and relaxation program as
an integral part of your **Personalized Stress
Management** program-design. Further suggestions can
be gained from consulting the previously cited book
by Friedman and Rosenman.

Part II.

STRESS COPING METHODS

CHAPTER 3.

Coping with Stress Cognitively

Cognitive methods of coping with stress are mental manipulations of our perceptions. They can be used in both negative (unhealthy) and positive (healthy) ways.

COGNITIVE COPING: NEGATIVE

Negative cognitive-coping methods are the excessive use of ego defense mechanisms in stressful situations. Ego defense mechanisms are cognitive devices that are used to mentally distort the reality of a stressful situation. Mental distortions reduce anxiety related to the situation while protecting the ego from a reality that is difficult to accept. Commonly used ego defense mechanisms are:

    1. **Repression** - This refers to the exclusion of unpleasant situations or experience from awareness. For instance, a student who has not studied for an upcoming exam may busy himself with other things that allow him to forget he has an exam.

    2. **Reaction formation** - This mechanism is obviously at work when someone goes overboard in expressing their objection to or innocence concerning an issue. The person who campaigns year after year for bills aimed against homosexuality, pickets

all homosexuality rallies, and has temper tantrums at any sign of their defense, may possibly have or is protecting latent homosexual fears of his own.

3. **Rationalization** - This refers to justifying one's actions or inactions with socially acceptable and logically possible reasons, as opposed to the real reason. Aesop's fable of "The Fox and the Grapes" is a good example of this mechanism at work. When the fox could not obtain some delicious-looking grapes, he decided that they were sour anyway.

4. **Projection** - This cognitive process is in action when one attributes his or her own denial or unwanted feelings and faults to someone else. To do so allows the person to focus on someone else as having the difficulty rather than himself. The person who is unable or embarrassed to show his own hostility is often quick to exaggerate the hostility of others. A woman threatened by her own sexual impulses may feel strongly that all men want from her is her body.

5. **Denial** - This refers to the process of ignoring or refusing to acknowledge the existence or significance of an unpleasant situation or experience. A person consistently putting on pounds may deny that he or she is gaining weight. Another example is the person who has been a chronic smoker or drinker who denies being addicted and claims he or she could quit whenever he wanted. The person may further deny that their addiction has any adverse effect on his health.

6. **Displacement** - This refers to shifting the expression of hostility, fear, or some other feeling from one person or object to a substitute that is safer and less threatening. A common example of this process is the father who is yelled at by his boss at work. He can not safely express his anger at his boss so he comes home and spanks his son. The son gets angry and kicks the dog. The dog gets angry and chases the cat.

7. **Withdrawal** - Withdrawal is an ego defense mechanism often associated with "copping out". It is most often used when a person perceives or realizes that a stressful situation or an adversary is more powerful than he or she; that there is no way he can change the situation; or that no compromise can be made.

Ego defense mechanisms are in many ways essential to the preservation of a healthy ego, and all functioning persons use them at some time or another. Used in moderation, they can help tide us over rough spots until we can deal more directly with a stressful problem. It is when we use them excessively, however, beyond apparent reality, that they become unhealthy and hazardous to our health. When used excessively or predominantly in coping with stress, they become self-defeating and self-deceptive and lead to a numbing effect in our awareness to both the stress and the amount of stress we are undergoing. This in turn prolongs the exposure to stress. The chronic smoker who is successful at denying that he or she is addicted, or that the smoking is affecting his health, may soon learn that he has a developing lung cancer and have difficulty breaking the habit. The denial mechanism may allow the person to escape the immediate anxiety related to the situation, but it does nothing to change or alleviate the problem situation.
==

REFLECTION

How often do you use the following defense
mechanisms. Circle the number that applies to you.

1 = very often   4 = not often
2 = often   5 = seldom
3 = sometimes

1.   Repression   1   2   3   4   5

2.   Reaction Formation   1   2   3   4   5

3.   Rationalization   1   2   3   4   5

4.   Projection   1   2   3   4   5

5.   Denial   1   2   3   4   5

6.   Displacement   1   2   3   4   5

7.   Withdrawal   1   2   3   4   5

There are no norms set for the frequency of using
ego defense mechanisms for coping with stress.
However, frequent or excessive use (very often and
often) should be minimized. Prolonged and
excessive use of these cognitive devices become
self-defeating in their purpose of relieving
stress.
==

COGNITIVE COPING: POSITIVE

a. Modifying perceptions

Our perceptions, both physical (sensual) and mental, give us information about our inner and outer worlds for a cognitive evaluation of how a situation will affect us. Our perception of a stressful event or situation involves an appraisal of the degree of its threats to our existent equilibrium. How we perceive a stressful event determines, to a large extent, how our minds and bodies will respond to it. Usually it is our first impression of a stressful event that is mentally exaggerated and, in most instances, irrational. By habit, in our initial perception of a stressful situation, many of us tend to catastrophize the intensity of the event. We blow it all out of proportion. If we are in pain , we are dying. If we lose our job, it the end of the world. This creates a defeatist attitude: we feel overwhelmed or unsuccessful before we begin to approach the situation. We waste all our energy over spilt milk without realizing that we may be able to get another glass.

By modifying our initial perception of a stressful event, cognitively, we can place the stressful situation in a more realistic and rational perspective. This in turn lowers the level of stress and decreases its effect on us both mentally and physically. The following steps are suggested for modifying perceptions:

1. List your first or initial perception of the event.

    a. Situation   b. Resulting feelings
    c. stress reaction

2. Modify your initial perception in more realistic and rational terms by reducing generalities and exaggerations.

```
          a. Situation    b. Resulting feelings
          c. Stress reaction
==================================================
```

REFLECTION:

Based on your initial perception, to cognitively
reduce stress related to a current or past
situation in your life, use the **Perception Chart**
that follows the example given below:

```
-----------------------------------------------------
```

Example:

1. Initial Perception

a. Situation: Refused a reasonable request: Giving
a stranded motorist a ride.

b. Consequential feelings   c. Stress reaction

(1)

I am a terrible, selfish   Guilt
person. I'm mean and
rejecting.

(2)

Someday I'll be refused   Feelings of insecurity
when I need a favor most.   and agitation.

2. Modified Perception

a. Situation: Refused a reasonable request: Needed to
get to work on time and didn't stop to give a stranded
motorist a ride.

b. Consequential feelings   c. Stress reaction

There have been many   I feel bad but not
times I have honored   overwhelmed by guilt.
reasonable and unreas-

<u>onable</u> <u>requests</u> <u>as</u> <u>well</u>.   _____

PERCEPTION CHART: Stressful Situations

1. Initial Perception

a. Situation: _____

_____

b. Consequential feelings   c. Stress reaction

_____   _____

_____   _____

_____   _____

2. Modified Perception

a. Situation: _____

_____

b. Consequential feelings   c. Stress reaction

_____   _____

_____   _____

_____   _____

===

b. Central focus adjustments

In addition to overexaggeration, another area where
our perceptions can cause added stress is, inappropriate focusing. Inappropriate focusing means
concentrating only, or predominantly, on the
adverse and noxious properties of a stressful
event. Focusing in this manner allows one negative
aspect of an event to dominate ten positive ones.
It adds stress to already existing stress by
delaying our decision-making process for taking
action. When decisions are made we go through
mental gymnastics over whether we made the right
choice or not. This encourages procrastination,
prolongs our exposure to stress, and promotes the
use of negative coping methods.

In many instances we can save ourselves from undue
stress by making adjustments in our focusing. This
can be done by balancing our thoughts (14) and
concentrating on both the negative and positive
aspects of our decisions. The best way to
accomplish this is by actually filling out a
thought balance sheet (see below). Balancing our
thoughts and concentration will help us act on our
decision by reducing the intensity of our focus on
the possible negative outcome. In this way,
procrastination is minimized, reducing the duration
of stress. The following steps are suggested for
decision making and thought balancing:

1. Describe the stressful situation.

2. List the decisions that could resolve
the problem.

3. List the negative aspects (outcomes) of
the decisions.

4. Balance the negative aspects of your decisions
by listing the positive aspects (outcomes).

===

REFLECTION:

To cognitively reduce stress related to a current or past situation, use the **Decision and Thought Balancing** chart that follows the example given below:

Example:

1. Stressful situation: Declining satisfaction with sex in my relationship.

2. Decision: Tell my partner.

3. Negative Aspects (outcomes):	4. Positive Aspects (outcomes):
It could hurt my partner's feelings. It could turn out to be my fault. It may jeopardize the relationship.	It could open new avenues of communication. The problem could be worked out in a supportive way. I'll be relieved once the problem is in the open. Taking a risk by sharing opens doors for growth in my relationship.

DECISION AND THOUGHT BALANCING CHART

1. Stressful situation: _____

----

2. Decision: _____

----

3. Negative aspects   4. Positive aspects
   (outcomes):   (outcomes):

_____   _____

_____   _____

_____   _____

_____   _____

_____   _____

==

Having a good repertoire of viable **positive** cognitive skills are very important part of your **Personalized Stress Management** program. Though they reside at a private and covert level, they have a definite influence on our social and overt behavior.

Negative cognitive coping methods are relatively harmless and often helpful if used in moderation. However, attempts should be made to keep them at a level of awareness, whereby we don't lose sight of how much and how long we are making use of them in specific stressful situations. If they are used exclusively and for long periods of time, they begin to work more against us than for us. It is to your benefit to keep negative cognitive coping as much as possible, a minimal part of our **Personalized Stress Management.**

CHAPTER 4.

Coping with Stress Actively

Active coping methods are direct physical actions taken to challenge, escape, avoid, or reduce stress or stressful situations. Like cognitive methods, they can be used in both negative (unhealthy) and positive (healthy) ways.

ACTIVE COPING: NEGATIVE

Negative active coping methods can be seen as readily available pacifiers, which people tend to reach for rather than seeking more direct means of resolving their difficulties and undesireable stressful situations. Pacifiers are not always unhealthy if used in moderation. An occasional glass of wine to relax in the evening or at dinner, or a snack break from work or chores has seldom done harm to anyone (unless they have an exceptional predisposition for addiction). It is only when pacifiers are used in excess that they become harmful and hazardous to our health. At which point they become crutches that we lean on to tide us over until the desireable situation takes care of itself.

It is not the direct purpose in this book to treat or manage negative active coping habits, so much as it is to teach positive active coping skills and how to use them effectively in managing stress. It is hoped, however, that the methods, when mastered, will alleviate or minimize the stress that leads to the use of negative active coping habits. If you find that you make excessive use of negative active coping habits, it is suggested that you approach the remainder of this chapter, and the stress management sections of this book, with the purpose of learning and developing positive habits to replace negative ones that are harmful and hazardous to your health.

==

REFLECTIONS:

How often do you use the following defense mechanisms? Circle the numer that applies to you.

1 = excessively   2 = moderately
3 = occasionally   4 = never

1.	Smoking	1	2	3	4
2.	Drinking	1	2	3	4
3.	Drugs and pills	1	2	3	4
4.	Overeating	1	2	3	4
5.	Sweets and snacks	1	2	3	4
6.	Others				
a.	_____	1	2	3	4
b.	_____	1	2	3	4
c.	_____	1	2	3	4
d.	_____	1	2	3	4

==

ACTIVE COPING: POSITIVE

Positive active-coping methods consist of various ways of preparing and conditioning the mind and body to sustain stress and increase vigor, and exploring available resources for dealing with stress. This can be done by developing a personalized relaxation, exercise, and nutrition program and being free to make use of the various resource systems available to you.

1. Relaxation

Relaxation is necessary for rejuvenation of mental and physical energy depleted by our thinking, anxieties, actions, and movements that are exerted throughout the day. It allows us to recharge our batteries before they are completely dead. During relaxation, the ratio of energy burned to energy produced by the body, is lower than when we are active.

In the course of a day (19), our body usually produces all the energy necessary for the next day. Depending upon our personalities, and the situation at hand , it is possible to burn a day's energy in a matter of minutes. When energy produced for a day is depleted in short periods of time, our body relies on its energy reserves. As we go into reserved energy, we become progressively more tired and less able to cope. Soon we reach a point whereby routine tasks become stressful, simply, because we do not have the energy to carry them out.

Of all stress coping methods, relaxation plays the most important role. Relaxaton is the antidote to stress. If you learn to relax yourself, while under a condition of stress, relaxation will serve to diminish the stress. It is impossible to be relaxed and stressed at the same time. By learning methods of relaxation, you will at the same time learn to control stress. Relaxation is the most direct means of immediate stress reduction, coping, or alleviation. Relaxation implies "letting go" of whatever occupies the mind and body, independently or together. In addition to tightened muscles, accelerated metabolism, and so forth, tension is caused by the body taking a tighter than normal grip on the mind. That is, under intensified situations there is an accelerated and more intense mental activity in the brain (mental associations) caused by our physical persistence of completing a task, resolving a problem or conflict, or escaping a situation that is threatening to our life or body. Often, even when we are physically removed from intensified situations, we continue to tax our mind and body with related worries and anxieties.

I am not suggesting that you learn to relax under conditions whereby there is a threat of bodily harm or losing your life, but you should learn to relax under day-to-day task completion and problem solving activities that cause tension, anxiety, and excessive wear and tear on the mind and body.

1. Specific methods and levels of relaxation

There are three levels of relaxation (1, 19): physical, mental, and spiritual. If accomplished in the order given, they will produce **complete** relaxation. When complete relaxation is obtained, we experience maximum tension release and stress reduction. There are several means of accomplishing each level of relaxation, including the use of chemical substances and mechanical devices. Through the methods to be described here, each level can be achieved naturally and without assistance.

Level I: Physical relaxation (progressive method)

For **physical relaxation**, the Jacobson progressive relaxation method is suggested. Progressive relaxation was used by Behavioral therapist, Joseph Wolpe (20), as an anxiety inhibitor in his

Reciprocal Inhibition methods of treating persons who suffered from phobias (irrational fears and anxieties). The principles of Reciprocal Inhibition contend that when a desirable response (relaxation) is successfully induced in the presence of an undesirable reaction (fear and anxiety), the desirable response will suppress the undesirable one. It further asserts that complete suppression is most likely to occur when the combination of conflicting fear-reaction and relaxation-response is introduced in a graded and systematic manner.

The similarity of these principles can be seen in the theory and methods of **progressive relaxation** to produce complete physical relaxation. Directives are given to exaggerate tension by tightening and squeezing the muscles, followed by counter instructions for relaxing the muscles and letting go. The process begins with the feet, and in a systematic manner, alternately tensing and relaxing each muscle group, progressing to the head and face. Upon completion, total physical relaxation is achieved.

Progressive relaxation can be practiced at any time and in almost any place, while driving, at the office or taking a break from a chore or activity for example. It is more beneficial, however, if practiced in the privacy of your home for a specified time and duration. You will have fewer distractions and gain fuller benefits from your accomplished relaxed state. Added effects will be facilitated if you actually set the scene for relaxation, such as a quiet or secluded place, dim lights, loose clothing, and if you like, some very soft relaxing music. Instructions for progressive relaxation are given below.

==

INSTRUCTIONS:

Choose a position that is comfortable to you. This could be lying flat on your back or sitting in an upright position in a comfortable chair with both feet on the floor and hands resting on your lap or arm rests. You should begin by developing a feeling of letting go and allowing your body to relax as fully as you can. Develop an awareness of your entire body and of how relaxed you feel. When you have relaxed to the best of your ability without moving, you are ready for progressive relaxation.

Begin with the feet. Be aware of your feet as separate from the rest of your body. Now clench your feet, pulling the toes in as tightly as you can. Now spread them as far apart as you can. Hold them in this position, then pull them inward again. Pull them in tighter and tighter until you can feel the tension.

When you have placed all the tension in your feet that you can, allow them to let go. Feel the relaxation coming in. Continue to relax your feet more and more. Feel the difference for a while, then move on to your legs and thighs. Begin by pushing them outward as far as you can (without moving your feet if seated). Tighten every muscle in your thighs and legs, stiffening them as much as you can. Hold your legs in this tensed position as long as you can, making every effort to increase the tension. Now feel yourself letting go. Feel your legs relaxing. Be aware of your control. Notice the difference between when they were tensed and when they were relaxed.

As you relax your legs, if you are not sure of your control, repeat the process again, tensing your legs and relaxing them, being aware of your control over tension and relaxation.

When you have done this, move on to your buttocks. Squeeze the cheeks of the buttocks together as tightly as possible. Be aware of the muscles in your buttocks. As you squeeze them, feel yourself rise from the floor or chair. See how far you can lift yourself by tightening these muscles more and

more.   Now let go of the tension in your buttocks.
Be as still as you can and allow the relaxation to
settle in.   Feel yourself becoming more and more
relaxed.   Notice that the lower half of your body
is now more relaxed than the upper half.   Be aware
that the upper half of your body awaits the
relaxation feeling accomplished by the lower half.

Now you may proceed to progressively relax the
upper half of your body, tensing and relaxing;
moving first to the abdominal region, moving on to
the chest, arms, shoulders; and then slowly move
upwards to the neck, head, and facial regions.   On
completion, be aware of your complete physical
relaxation.
==

Level II: Mental Relaxation (complete-breathing
            method)

For **mental relaxation**, the method of complete
breathing is recommended.   **Complete breathing**
maximizes the expansion of your lungs such that you
are able to absorb maximum oxygen intake.   Complete
breathing increases the exchange of oxygen and
carbon in the body whereby augmenting oxygenation.
This process serves to soothe the mind, giving a
light and floating sense of mental relaxation.

Yoga (1, 14) distinguishes between three methods of
breathing: (1) low breathing, breathing from the
diaphragm (2) medium breathing, breathing from the
chest and (3) high breathing, breathing from the
shoulders.   Diaphragmatic breathing gives you more
oxygen than chest breathing does; chest breathing
takes in more oxygen than shoulder breathing takes
in.   Shoulder breathing gives you the least amount
of oxygen.   In chest and shoulder breathing, the
abdomen contracts during inhalation, minimizing
your lung's intake of air.   Conversely, in
diaphragmatic breathing, the stomach pushes out,
lowering the diaphragm, increasing the capacity of
the lungs, and allowing more air intake.

Diaphragmatic breathing is generally referred to as deep breathing. When asked to breath deeply, most people use chest and shoulder breathing. Both are inferior to breathing from the diaphragm. Though diaphragmatic breathing is a natural process, it must be learned and practiced on a regular basis to make use of it naturaly when we want to deliberately increase or maximize our oxygen intake.

Neither of the breathing methods used exclusively will give us **complete breathing**. Complete breathing requires the use of all three methods in progression: low, medium, and high breathing in a continuous motion, as in taking a single breath, giving maximum oxygen intake. Maximum intake of oxygen soothes the mind, and gives a floating sensation. Breathing this way generates a feeling of peace and harmony and relaxes and calms the mind.

===

INSTRUCTIONS:

To learn **complete breathing**, you should first master all three breathing methods: diaphragmatic (abdominal), chest, and shoulder breathing.

Abdominal breathing

Begin by lying flat on your back. Place both hands lightly over your stomach. Breath so that you can feel your stomach pushing your hands up. Do not move your chest and shoulders. Breath slowly and evenly, counting forward as you inhale.

Keeping track of the number you reach, hold your breath about one-half second, then begin to exhale slowly, counting backwards from the number you reached to zero. The number you reached while inhaling can be used to make comparisons of oxygen intake when you practice chest and shoulder breathing.

Another way to practice abdominal breathing, is to sit in a chair with the spine, neck, and head straight. Place your left hand on your chest and the right on the stomach. Relax the abdominal muscles. Use your left hand to prevent your chest from expanding. You should not raise the shoulders. Now, breathe so that you feel the stomach pushing your right hand outward. Again, breathe slowly and evenly, counting forward as you inhale. Keep track of the number you reach. Hold your breath about one-half second, then exhale slowly, counting backwards from the number you reached to zero. Practice abdominal breathing until you have mastered it.

Chest breathing

Practice chest breathing by sitting in an erect position, with the diaphragm still. That is, do not allow the abdomen to expand. Next, expand the chest and begin to inhale slowly and evenly, taking in as much air as you can. As you breathe, count forward as far as you can. Keep track of the number you reach, hold your breath for about one-half second. Next begin to exhale slowly, counting backwards to zero. Compare chest and abdominal breathing by the numbers you reached when counting forward for each exercise.

Practice chest breathing until you have mastered it and begin practicing shoulder breathing.

Shoulder breathing

Practice shoulder breathing by sitting in an erect position, with the spine and neck straight. Contract the abdomen by holding the stomach muscles tightly. Begin inhaling as much air as you can by raising the shoulders and collar bone. Breathe slowly and evenly and count forward, keeping track of the number you reach.

When you have taken in as much air as you can, hold your breath about one-half second and begin to exhale slowly, counting backwards to zero. Compare shoulder breathing with abdominal and chest breathing. Practice shoulder breathing until you have mastered it.

Complete Breathing

When you have mastered all three breathing methods individually, you are ready to learn **complete breathing.**

Employ the following steps to master complete breathing. (1) Breath slowly and evenly to inhale as much air as you can into your lungs, by pushing the stomach out {abdominal breathng}. (2) Without exhaling, expand the chest and take in more air {chest breathing}. (3) Lift the shoulders and collar bone and take in still more air {shoulder breathing}. (4) Hold your breath about one-half second. (5) Begin exhaling slowly and evenly by letting the shoulders and collar bone down. (6) Slowly relax the chest. (7) Gradually constrict the abdomen by tightening your stomach muscles.

Repeat this procedure twice. When you have done so, you will have completely emptied the lungs with old air and filled them with fresh, new air. This is complete breathing.

Practice complete breathing until you have mastered it. Once you have done so, you will find that complete breathing will be helpful in easing your tension in all stressful situations, by cooling and relaxing the mind. If you practice on a regular basis, you will develop a conditioned habit, whereby in stressful moments you will trigger a complete breathing reflex.

Level III: Spiritual Relaxation

Spiritual relaxation is complete relaxation. It is the highest form of relaxation and can only be achieved after our bodies and minds are relaxed. When both are relaxed, the mind has the potential to transcend, and withdraw its concentration from the demands of the body and the physical world around us, and has the freedom to dwell on its all-prevailing, all-peaceful, omnipotent, and joyful self.

A popular method of achieving spiritual relaxation is the Yogic method of transcendental meditation (TM). Were you to take training in TM, you would be privately interviewed by an instructor and assigned a mantra. Mantras are special sounds (e.g. **om, ieng, ah nam,** to name a few) that reflects your character and profession. Your mantra is private and a pledge to its secrecy is encouraged. To meditate, you settle down for a half minute or so, and close your eyes. Repeat the mantra to yourself over and over again for a period of fifteen to twenty minutes. By doing so, you develop a passive attitude and drift into a trance or trance-like state. This allows your mind to transcend the external world and identify with its universal self. Meditating twice per day is general practice for TM practitioners.

For many Westerners, the Eastern (Yogic) methods of achieving higher levels of relaxation is viewed as much too unorthodox and mystical for experimental practice. If you are skeptical of TM, but have some curiosity, it might be interesting to note that extensive studies in the United States (2, 4) have demonstrated that one doesn't have to adopt Eastern doctrines or exclusive Yogic practices to benefit from their conceptual inductive methods of higher levels of relaxation, and the use of mantras are not essential. Repeating a simple word such as <u>relax</u> or the number <u>one</u> over and over, or concentrating on your breathing for extended periods of time will suffice to elicit a desired state of higher-level relaxation. The schedule and length of time of your practice can be set according to your personal conveniences.

How you achieve spiritual relaxation is really a matter of preference. Many are able to achieve it through religion and prayers; others through philosophical literature that contains knowledge for the sake of knowledge. However you achieve it, the experience provides nourishment for the mind and contributes to your inner strength.

(2) General Methods of Relaxation

In addition to specific relaxation exercises, your relaxation program should include general methods of relaxation, such as massage, general creative activity, vacations, and warm baths as well. General methods are equally important and helpful in achieving relaxation. It should be included as a part of your **PSM** rest and relaxation program as provided for in Chapter 7.

2. Nutrition

Good nutrition plays an essential role in our ability to cope with stress. It is the source through which we receive the necessary materials to produce the energy we need to function. Like a machine, the body does not run without proper fuel. The body is much more sophistiated than a machine and is able to perform an abundance of functions that are incomparable and require a greater variety of energy sources. There is no machine that can program itself or be programmed to match the number, variety, and often quality of performances and functions of the body. Much of the body's advantage over a machine is accounted for by its autogeneous ability to self-process, manufacture, and produce the special kinds of energy necessary to perform the wealth of activities of which it is capable.

Whatever function we engage in, running, thinking, sitting, eating, feeling, talking, and so on, every

action and inaction requires a particular kind of
energy. In order to produce the specialized energy
it needs, the body must be supplied with the proper
raw materials. They are called nutrients and
consist of proteins, carbohydrates, lipids (fats),
minerals and vitamins (6). If these nutrients are
not available, the body will not function at its
fullest potential. Principal supplies of different
nutrients are found in different sources of foods.
Your diet should include a variety of foods from
all four food groups: (1) Milk and milk products,
butter, cheeses, etc.; (2) Meats, eggs, beans, and
other basic protein sources; (3) Fruits,
vegetables, and nuts; and (4) breads, cereals, and
grain products.

The nutritional value and potency of these foods
depend on what happens to them before they are
actually consumed by the body. Whether they were
produced artificially, chemically, or a combination
of the two; how they were processed (refined, use
of preservatives, dyes, bleaches, hydrolized or
dehydrated, homogenized or pasteurized); and how
they were prepared (canned, glassed, frozen,
seasoned, cooked, overcooked, or fastcooked).
Naturally and organically grown and produced foods
that are fresh and have little or no commercial
processing, carefully prepared with minimal cooking
and use of seasoning, will preserve the nutritional
value of foods. Commercially produced or processed
foods, overcooked foods, fast food production, and
over-seasoned foods deplete the vitamin value and
should be avoided.

Although vitamins are not an actual energy source,
they do regulate the body's use of minerals, which
go into the production of energy and their presence
is absolutely essential for proper cell and tissue
metabolism, their growth and preservation.

Some of the principal vitamins are: A, B and B
complex, C, D, E, and K. Each of these vitamins
play a particular role in their importance to
particular systems and organs of the body, such as

glandular, respiratory, hormonal, kidney, liver, sense organs, and so forth. Some are important to all.

Vitamins play a role in our overall resistance to disease and play an important role in our tolerance for stress. Every organ and system of our body is effected when an individual is under stress. Under normal living conditions, our body uses vitamins in small quantities. Under stessful conditions, our rate of metabolism is accelerated, and may deplete our overall vitamin supply more rapidly than is normal. Additionally, we tend to lose our appetite and eat less. When under stress, we pay less attention to the nutritional content and value of what we eat, and junk foods, fast foods, sweets, and alcoholic beverages appear more attractive.

Unlike other standard organic nutrients (carbohydrates, fats, proteins) we consume, the body cannot synthesize vitamins when it is vitamin-deficient. This is unfortunate because vitamins are so much more easily destroyed through food preparation. A single cooking can sometimes destroy fifty percent or more of the vitamin nutrients (15). You can imagine the overall loss when food is overly seasoned, recooked, or reheated.

Because our body cannot synthesize vitamins, we must include them in our diet. In our hurry scurry urban life, it is difficult for the average person to get enough vitamins from his daily diet. Because of this and the ever growing decrease in the nutritional value of foods we consume, it becomes increasingly important that you supplement your diet with extra vitamins. Vitamins that are closely connected with building and maintaining stress resistance are B and B-Complex. These vitamins are more directly associated with the facilitation of our mental, brain, and nerve functioning. Minerals that augment their potency are iron, magnesium, and manganese. I recommend the following practices to help ensure proper nutrition.

1. Be sure that your diet is well balanced, consisting of a good variety of the four food groups mentioned earlier.

2. Be conscious of the nutritional value of the foods you consume and how they are prepared.

3. Trim your meats of excess fat, but avoid or minimize peeling and trimming your fruits and vegetables as much as possible. In most fruits and vegetables there is a greater concentration of vitamins and minerals in the skins and tops than in the body. Meat fats are known for causing cholesterol buildup in the body that interfere with blood passage. To meet your needs for oils and fats, use those that are of vegetable origin, for example, salad, corn, olive, peanut, sunflower, and so forth.
==

REFLECTION:

How knowledgeable are you of the nutritional needs of your body?

	Yes	No
(1) Do you have a nutritional breakfast to start off your day?	_____	_____
(2) Are you a fast eater?	_____	_____
(3) Are you satisfied with your eating habits?	_____	_____
(4) Are you overweight? If so, do you know why?	_____	_____
(5) Do you know the vitamin, mineral, and protein content		

of the various foods you eat?   _____   _____

(6) Do you have a nutritional
    program?   _____   _____

===

3. Exercise

Exercise can serve both **as an end,** in and of
itself, and a **means to and end** (6), for actively
coping with stress.

a. Exercise: As an End

Exercise **as an end** can serve as an outlet for the
indirect expression of emotions, and can aid in the
relaxation of specific muscles and muscle groups
that are tense from prolonged and unresolved
stress.

Primitive man had to move in order to work.
Exercise was a natural requirement for survival.
Most of his working day was spent out of doors and
there was less mental activity that required the
suppression of emotion. Modern workers on the
other hand are more confined, both physically and
mentally, with jobs that often require us to sit
still on a daily basis for prolonged periods of
time. Frequently, we are confined to close places,
with limited physical movement and emotional
expression. In the process, we are forced to
inhibit our natural reactions. Our muscles or
various muscle systems continually go into a state
of preparation to act, but we do not act. Over a
period of time, our emotions build up and tensions
accumulate in certain muscles and muscle groups
which absorb the suppressed apprehensions and
inhibited arousals. As a result, we become tense.

Accumulated tensions in specific areas of the body
can serve as indicators of over-stress. These
indicators are the body's natural early warning

signs and should be seen as beneficial. They should be acknowledged and attended to. They should not be seen as nuisances to be denied, ignored, or smothered. We should learn to make these signs work for us. If the stress itself cannot be alleviated, we should at least give attention to the particular areas of the body that are absorbing the tensions.

For many people, accumulated tensions that serve as stress indicators frequently arise in the shoulders, neck, and back. For others, tension causes the sudden or gradual onset of a headache. Various exercises that will reduce accumulated tension in these stress indicator areas will follow.

==

REFLECTION:

What are your stress indicators?

What attention do you give them?

1. _____   _____

2. _____   _____

3. _____   _____

4. _____   _____

5. _____   _____

==

b. Exercises for Stress Indicators

When early warning signs are ignored for too long, we become insensitive to their existence, subjecting ourselves and our bodies to stress beyond our endurance. This could lead to sudden burnout or exhaustion.

To relieve tension in specific areas of the body where signs of being over-stressed are first exhibited, stretch and posture exercises are recommended. Such exercises not only release uptight feelings for the moment, they also provide increased elasticity and produce flexibility which increases our tolerance for stress in tensed areas. If we practice the recommended exercises often enough, we will become accustomed to the flexibility and elasticity in our muscles, such that our awareness of tension and stiffness will be more apparent, and we will be more encouraged to give them the attention they need.

Stretching and posture exercises also improve the functioning of the entire nervous system and in turn reduce the likelihood of headaches.

The exercises suggested here are relatively simple and less strenuous than many that are given in Yogic and Chiropractic traditions. They are by no means offered as a substitute for the actual practice of either discipline. They will suffice, however, as a method of giving adequate attention to early warnings signs of stress. These exercises are not to be practiced in a fast manner, as in calisthenics or competitive sports. The idea in stretching and posture exercises is to see how smoothly and rhythmetically you can attain the suggested position, how far you can stretch into the position, and how long you can maintain the position without prolonged undue discomfort.

It is not expected that you will attain the full position in the beginning phases of your practice. But the more frequently you practice the exercises in the prescribed fashion, the more fully you will be able to attain the suggested position, and the longer you will be able to maintain it without discomfort.

The key to maximum benefits from stretching exercises is deep (diaphragmatic) breathing; inhaling as much air as you can when stretching, and exhaling (emptying the lungs as much as possible) when letting go.

Practice deep breathing, at least ten times while in each suggested posture. This is a good baseline for completing most of the suggested exercises. If you are a beginner, you may want to start with a baseline of five cycles of total inhalation and exhalation (deep breathing) for each exercise completion.

==

Illustrations: Exercises for stress
indicators and early warning signs

==

1. GENERAL   TENSION RELEASE:

(a) Skeleton Dance   (b) Forward Droop

2. NECK AND SHOULDER TENSION RELEASE:

(a) Head Nod and Roll   (b) Shoulder Roll
(c) Arms Roll   (d) Shoulder Stand

3. NECK, SHOULDER, AND BACK TENSION RELEASE

(a) Plow Position   (b) Fish Pose

4. NECK AND BACK TENSION RELEASE

(a) Locust Pose

5. BACKACHES AND TENSION RELEASE

(a) Cobra Pose   (b) Knee to Chest

6. COMPLETE RELAXATION AND TENSION RELEASE

(a) Corpse Pose

GENERAL TENSION RELEASE

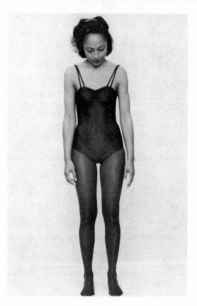

Skeleton Dance

Instructions:

Stand in as relaxed a position as you can. Allow
your head to fall forward and shoulders to droop,
arms and hands to dangle to your sides, and the
entire body to droop and feel limp. While in this
position, raise yourself up and down using the balls
of your feet in a continuous bouncing motion. Do
this bouncing motion about 100 times, allowing the
body and limbs to dangle, dance, and shake like a
skeleton dangling on a string.

Benefits: General tension release, relaxes and
loosens up the whole body, and gives a feeling of
letting go.

Forward Droop

Instructions:

From a standing position, keeping the legs straight, bend forward and allow the head, arms, and hands to droop. Hold this position and be as relaxed as you can. Allow the arms to dangle. Then inhale, taking a deep breath. As you exhale, push your arms and hands downward toward your feet as far as it is comfortable and hold that position. Then inhale again. As you exhale, attempt to push downward a bit further. Now relax and hold this position as long as it is comfortable for you. Then return to your original standing position. If you feel uncomfortable at this point, place your hands on your hips and allow yourself to bend backwards a bit. This will counter the forward bending to give a more complete relaxed feeling.

Benefits: General tension release, good for back aches, and gives a relaxed feeling of letting go.

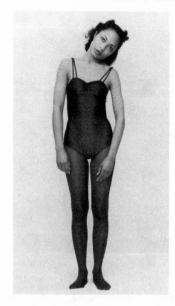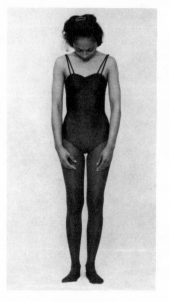

Head Nod and Roll

Instructions:

Sit or stand with head upright and shoulders relaxed, and arms hanging loosely to the sides. In a smooth, slow and deliberate motion, nod your head to the left shoulder and return to head upright position; nod your head to the right shoulder, and return to head upright position. Nod your head to the chest, and return to the head upright position; Next, lean your head backwards, and return to head upright position. Then lean your head to the left shoulder and very slowly roll the neck clockwise in a complete circle. Without raising the head, roll it very slowly in the opposite direction, counterclockwise. Return the head to an upright position. Repeat the entire exercise two or three times.

Benefits: Releases tension and relaxes the muscles in the neck and shoulders.

Shoulder Roll

Instructions:

Sit or stand with head upright, and arms hanging loosely to the sides. Raise the shoulders high. In a slow and smooth motion, roll the shoulders forward in a circular motion about five or six times. Then roll the shoulders in the same manner in a reverse circular motion. Alternate forward and reverse shoulder rolling about three or four times.

Benefits: Releases tension and relaxes the neck and shoulder muscles. Also relieves headache tensions.

Arms Roll

                    Instructions:
Stand with legs slightly parted, bending forward,
and arms stretched forward: (1) with head hanging
loosely in a downward position, in a free swing
circle bring the arms up, back and forward again.
(2) Do this circular motion twenty times. (3) In
the same position, with head raised, do this same
exercise in a reverse motion twenty times.

Benefits: Relieves cramps and pain in the neck and
shoulders and relaxes the neck and shoulder muscles.

Shoulder Stand

Instructions:

Lie on the floor flat on your back. Slowly raise the legs until they are aligned in a vertical position with the trunk and hips. Rest the elbows on the floor, and support the back with both hands. Keep the chin tucked against the chest and breath slowly and evenly. Stay in this position as long as it is comfortable, keeping the whole weight of your body on your shoulders to avoid discomfort. When the position becomes uncomfortable, return to the original position, lying flat on your back. Practice three cycles of complete breathing and rest quietly for a few seconds.

Benefits: Relieves tension in the back and neck muscles, stretches the spine and improves circulation in all body parts and tones the nervous system.

Plow Position

Instructions:

Not recommended for persons with acute hernia or back problems.

Lie on the floor flat on your back, placing the palms of the hands under the buttocks for support. Keeping the legs straight, slowly swing the feet over beyond the head until the toes touch the floor. Slowly breath through the nose, pressing the chin against the chest. Remain in this position as long as it is comfortable and return to a lying flat position. Do not try to force yourself to touch the floor with your toes. If you are a beginner, this will be very difficult. The more you practice this exercise the more limber your spine will become and the easier it will be to reach the floor. As a starter, you can go back far enough to rest your knees on your forehead.

Benefits: Good for tight back and neck muscles, and helps relieve headaches.

Fish Pose

Instructions:

Lie down flat on your back with legs together and extended. Place the hands, palms down, under the buttocks. Arch the back and allow the upper half of the body to rest on your elbows with the top of the head leaning back and resting on the floor. Retain this position about sixty seconds or longer while deep breathing.

Benefits: Relieves stiffness in the neck and middle back. Relaxes neck and shoulder muscles while increasing circulation.

Locust Pose

Instructions:

Lie face down on the floor, with the arms and hands close beside the body. Turn the palms upward and make a tight fist. Raise the head and rest the chin on the floor. Stiffen the whole body. With legs together and straight, lift the legs as high as you can. Take a deep breath, hold it, then exhale and gently lower the legs to the floor. Repeat this exercise three times. If you are a beginner, you may not be able to raise both legs at once on the first try. As a beginner, practice this exercise by raising one leg at a time.

Benefits: Good for backaches and stiffness of the neck. Strengthens the muscles and increases circulation.

CAUTION: Not recommended for persons with acute hernia and back problems.

Cobra Pose

Instructions:

Allow the entire body to relax as much as possible. Lie flat on your stomach with the toes extended. Place the hands, palms down under the shoulders. In a slow and smooth manner, raise the head and upper portion of the body, bending the spine well and arching the back as far as you can without lifting the navel from the floor. As you raise your body to an arched position, inhale slowly and feel each vertebrae of the spine, bending one at a time. Hold your breath as you retain this position. Stretch as much as you can. Now begin exhaling and lowering the body slowly to the floor, feeling each vertebrae level out one by one until you are lying flat on the floor again. Repeat this exercise about four or five times.

Benefits: Relieves backaches, limbers the spine, and tones the back muscles.

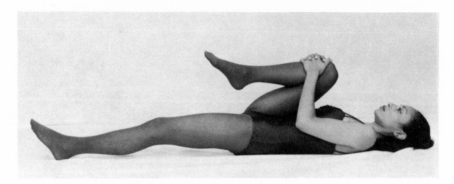

Knee to Chest

Instructions:

Lie flat on your back. Bring the right knee to the chest with the hands folded around the knee. Take a deep breath. Hold it in while pressing the knee as hard as you can against the chest. Hold your breath for as long as you can. Release the right knee and repeat the same exercise with the left knee. Next, release the left knee and repeat the same exercise with both knees together. Before releasing both knees, take a deep breath, hold your breath and rock gently back and forth. Do the entire sequence of exercises three times.

Benefits: Good for back problems, relieves stiffness and soreness of the back, massages the spine.

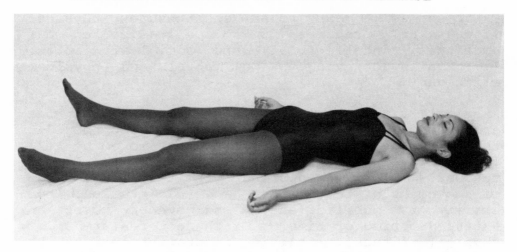

Corpse Pose

Instructions:

Lie flat on your back. Head and spine straight, arms lying flat just away from the body and palms turned upward. Legs are straight and heels slightly apart. Allow the body to feel as completely relaxed and limp as you can. Practice complete breathing five times to allow yourself to feel floating sensations, and a sense of calm and total relaxation. Lie in this position for fifteen minutes or longer.

Benefits: Complete mental and physical relaxation. Good for back aches and headaches.

b. Exercise: As a means to an End

Exercise **as a means to an end** ensures physical
fitness and prepares us to capitalize on our
emotional, intellectutal, and social attributes.
It aids in achieving maximum mental and physical
efficiency.

Physical fitness can be broken down into three
areas of functioning: (1) strength, which provides
the basic muscular force required for movement; (2)
flexibility, that quality of muscles, bones,
tendons, and ligaments that permit the full range
of movement of the joints; and (3) stamina, our
ability to mobilize energy and movement over an
extended period of time. Of these three areas of
physical fitness, training in stamina tend to be
the most vital form of adult exercise, and it is
well within the capabilities of all adults
regardless of age.

An overall exercise program should include exercises for training in flexibility and strengthening, as well as stamina. For instance, if we
choose running, calisthenics, or brisk walking as
our standard stamina-building exercise, we should
also use flexibility exercise such as bending and
stretching, and strengthening exercises such as
pushups and knee bends as both pre- and post-
exercise warmups and settling down.

The overall benefit of exercise, in addition to
physical fitness, is that it increases our resil-
iency and resistance to stress. In addition to
building up our resistance to stress, it helps to
keep our weight in control, inhibits premature
aging and physical deterioration, and, in general,
helps us look and feel younger.

Everyone, regardless of age should be involved in
an exercise program. If you do not already have a
routine exercise program, Chapter 7 is designed to
help you establish an exercise program to meet your
individual needs.

4. Support Systems

A good support system is one that allows us to share our worries, anxieties, and pain in appropriate ways. This means being able to share the right things in the right places at the right times. It is just not appropriate to share anything with anybody at any time. Sharing in this way becomes more self-defeating than self-relieving.

For instance, if our spouse is the limit of our support system and we have worries concerning our job or other difficulties that are of no direct concern to our spouse, often the most he/she will be able to offer us is blind assurances such as "don't worry, everything will be all right", or "I'm sure it will work itself out". Often these remarks will increase our anxiety rather than help alleviate it. This happens mainly because we do not feel that we have been truly understood. The person we are sharing with either cannot relate to the problem or has no direct concern in it. They, therefore, tend to either minimize or over exaggerate the seriousness of the matter being discussed. We also run the risk of overburdening our spouse with matters that do not directly concern them, leaving them little energy for matters that do.

In order to share in appropriate ways, you must have a broad support system that allows you to share only where there is direct concern. When our support system is too narrow to meet our sharing needs, our sharing results in support system overload, abuse, and eventually, burnout. If we have concerns that are job-related, perhaps they should be shared with our employer and/or fellow employees; if we have marital difficulties, perhaps they should be shared with our spouse, close friend, or professional counselor; or if we have a problem with a relative, perhaps it should be shared with another relative.

In any event, it is important to remember that stress is easier to tolerate when it is shared with other concerned individuals. Sharing the problem is also sharing the burden. Difficulties are much more devastating when one has to suffer the burden alone, without support.

Relaxation, good nutrition, proper exercise, and appropriate support systems for sharing are all the proper ingredients for positive means of coping with stress in an active way. Active coping methods are definitely more effective than cognitive ones. They provide more direct and deliberate means of controlling and reducing the impact of stress, and the possibility of self-deception tends to be less. Equally important, active coping methods prepare us to deal with unexpected stress and keeps us in stress-ready condition.

The effectiveness of positive active coping methods depends not only on the skills and habits we develop in using such methods, but also on the prescribed manner in which they are applied. The remaining chapters of this book are designed to improve your effectiveness in using **positive** active coping skills and develop habits of managing stress through providing a carefully designed program for their application in everyday life and work.

With the understanding of stress gained in Part I of this book, together with the recent development of coping skills provided in Part II which includes preparation and stress-ready conditioning, we are now ready for the final and most important stage of **Personalized Stress Management** (a **PSM** program). The PSM program is covered in the remaining chapters (Part III) and will give practical application of your understanding of stress and develop skills for coping.

Part III.

STRESS MANAGEMENT PROGRAM

CHAPTER 5.

Program Design and Mental Conditioning

The development of an individualized program lies at the heart of **Personalized Stress Management (PSM)**. It provides organization, facilitation, and coordination of all the material we have covered thus far. A **PSM** program is the production of a strategy or plan that will allow us to get maximum results from minimum expenditures of energy in our pursuits of desired goals in life. It is a means of economizing stress, and making more effective and efficient use of our time and energy.

By setting up a **PSM** program, we save the energy wasted in hit-and-miss, trial-and-error, and self-defeating avoidance methods of dealing with stress. In the process, we are taking definite steps designed for definite results. This means that we are in control of what is taking place in all aspects of our lives, career, social, personal, or otherwise. We are also setting limits and controlling the duration of whatever stress we encounter.

Having a **PSM** program creates and maintains an awareness of not only stressful situations in our lives, but also the amount of time and energy that we have available to deal with them. When we develop a viable **PSM** program, we create an overall consciousness of our lives and how we are prepared to live it. In the process, stress becomes more of a challenge than a burden.

This chapter is devoted to the description and design for developing a **PSM** program. Mental conditioning, the first of six steps in a successful program is also covered. The remaining five steps of the program are presented in the chapters that follow.

PSM PROGRAM DESIGN

The six steps in setting up a **Personalized Stress management** program are:

(1) Mental Conditioning

(2) Organization and Time Energy Assessment

(3) Goal Assessment for each aspect of life

(4) Decision and Planning

(5) Plan Implementation

(6) Evaluation

===

PSM PROGRAM SCHEMATIC VIEW:

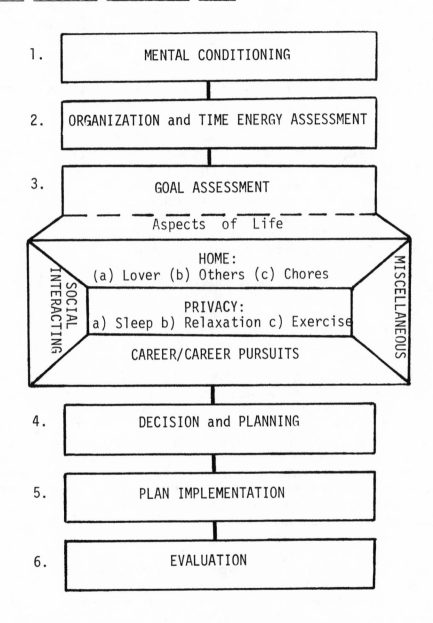

1. | MENTAL CONDITIONING

2. | ORGANIZATION and TIME ENERGY ASSESSMENT

3. | GOAL ASSESSMENT

Aspects of Life

SOCIAL INTERACTING

HOME:
(a) Lover (b) Others (c) Chores

PRIVACY:
a) Sleep b) Relaxation c) Exercise

CAREER/CAREER PURSUITS

MISCELLANEOUS

4. | DECISION and PLANNING

5. | PLAN IMPLEMENTATION

6. | EVALUATION

===

MENTAL CONDITIONING

In addition to competence (knowledge, understanding, and skill) the key to success in any plan, triumph, or goal is to develop the confidence that you are going to succeed and to believe this so strongly that all your concentration and energy goes into succeeding. If no energy is wasted on worry and anxiety or fear of failure, the momentum for success remains constant, and you require less energy as you proceed toward your objective.

Very few people win by surprise. Most people who win have strong feelings that they are going to win, and have a definite plan to do so. Athletes are well aware of this. In addition to their physical conditioning, they go into a game or event mentally prepared to win. Losing is the last thought to enter their minds.

As in sports, there are winners and losers in life. There are those who are mentally conditioned to win and have a strategy or plan to do so; and then there are those who just play around and hope for a surprise victory.

Mental conditioning calls for developing an atti-attitude of self- assuredness and confidence, placing our inner selves at the locus of control over our lives. For many people, such mental conditioning is termed "psyching yourself up." It is like developing a natural high that gives us a positive feeling about ourselves. Many of us are able to gain this feeling with little effort, but for others it takes training and discipline. In either case, it is an ability that can be developed or improved in all of us.

Mental conditioning is a spiritual endeavor and as with spiritual relaxation, how it is practiced is a matter of preference. Many people practice it through prayer, meditation, and groups that lend positive support. Others have developed their own private means. One method I would like to talk about here is hypnosis.

a. Hypnosis

To many people, hypnosis is a mysterious and taboo
subject. Most of the mystery and fear regarding
hypnosis stems from lack of information and
misconceptions that are Hollywood productions. If,
you asked anyone who has actually experienced
hypnosis what it was like, I am sure they would
report that it was a very pleasant and relaxing
experience.

In a sense, hypnosis is nothing out of the
ordinary. To a degree, we all practice it every
day without being aware of it. Though we may not
experience an actual hypnotic trance, we do enter
into trance-like captivity when we allow ourselves
to concentrate on a subject (person, place, or
thing, real or imagined) to the extent that we are
oblivious to our environment.

How often have you heard a woman say, "When my
husband sits down in front of the television, and
there is a ball game on, a herd of wild horses
couldn't drag him away". Or a man say, "When my
wife is on the phone, the house could go up in
flames, and she would never know it." These people
are describing states similar to hypnosis. Unlike
being in an actual state of hypnosis, however, the
captivity the man and woman are experiencing could
be broken by a simple, rather abrupt, change in
their existant physical state of being, even if it
was suggested that nothing would disturb them.

Imagine that woman suggested to her husband while
he was deeply engrossed in the ball game, "I am
going to pour this tall glass of cold water over
your head, and you won't feel a thing"; Or the man
suggested to his wife. "I'm going to prick the tip
of your finger with this pin I have in my hand and
you will never know it happened." If they carried
out such actions, there is little doubt that they
would get each other's attention. Were they in an

actual state of hypnosis, however, the suggestions
given would have been taken more as if they were a
reality, and the responses given would have been as
such. The man and woman were more in a state of
concentration rather than one of hypnosis. A
similarity to be noted concerning the two states is
that in either condition, if the experience is not
enjoyable or desired, the person can terminate the
experience at will.

Hypnosis is described as an altered state of
consciousness. Consciousness is understood to be
our normal everyday waking state. When we are in
our normal everyday waking state, we are alert
mentally and physically and are aware of our
environment in relation to ourselves. Hypnosis is
but one of several conditions under which our
consciousness can be altered. Other conditions
consist of chemical and drug influences,
meditation, and various stages of sleep. Hypnosis
can be differentiated by its paradoxical effect.

When under hypnosis, though you are neither asleep
or awake, your mind is active and alert as if
awake, but your body is relatively inanimate, as if
asleep. When in this state, you feel like an
outside participant in whatever mental activity
that is taking place. It is like a dream, but not
a dream. Perhaps it would be better understood as
an intensely captivating day-dream, that is
maintained by stimulated imagination. When under
hypnosis, your awareness is heightened; perceptions
are keener, more vivid, and less limited than when
in a waking state; and your defense system relaxes,
increasing your susceptibility to suggestion,
especially if the person making the suggestions is
someone you trust.

For our purposes here of mental conditioning, the
use of hypnosis will be confined to self-hypnosis.
Besides being more convenient, it will contribute
to a growing sense of self-reliance. The goal of
self-hypnosis will be to place yourself in a
relaxed state of mind, increasing your

susceptibility to conditioning suggestions of confidence and commitment given to yourself.

b. Self-hypnosis

Essentially, self-hypnosis follows the same principles of progressive relaxation and reciprocal inhibition given in Chapter Four. It differs in its ultimate objective, however, which is to produce a state of self-induced relaxation-trance or deep relaxation-captivity that will increase your receptiveness to self-suggestion. This extends beyond the goals of physical relaxation per se, as in traditional progressive relaxation.

The principles of self (or other induced) hypnosis implies that (1) if in the presence of a normal state of alertness, (2) a counteracting deep state of relaxation is successfully induced, (3) when the conflicting conditions become equal (one directly oppposing the other), (4) an alternate state, a relaxation trance is produced, and (5) your vulnerability to suggestion is more than usual.

There are several methods to achieve hypnosis through self-induction. In my practice, the one I have found to work best and easiest to learn for most of my clients is a modified version of progressive relaxation. The continued uninterrupted suggestions of relaxation will more easily overcome your alert state to produce a relaxation trance of self-hypnosis.

The procedure consists of (1) mentally giving yourself a statement of suggestion in regards to relaxation taking place in a certain area of your body; and (2) pausing a few seconds to allow the body to follow through on the mental facilitation of the suggestion to gain a state of self-hypnosis. Complete mental concentration is used to relax yourself without physical effort or assistance. To minimize interference in your concentration memorize the procedure and instructions well.

==

INSTRUCTIONS: SELF INDUCTION

To begin, find yourself a secluded place where you
will not be disturbed. Position yourself in a
chair with your back and spine straight. Rest your
feet flat on the floor, your arms and hands on your
lap or arm rest, and with your eyes gently closed,
look upward as though there were a spot on your
forehead. Soothe your mind through the **complete-
breathing** method (see chapter four). Breath
completely three times, relax, and allow the mind
to cool. Be aware of the floating sensations.
Then repeat the following instructions to yourself,
pausing (...) where indicated:

"As I sit here in this chair, with both feet flat
on the floor, I find my feet growing heavier and
heavier.....The heaviness of my feet are now moving
up into my legs and thighs, giving them a very
relaxed feeling...Now my buttocks and hips are
growing heavy, and the entire lower half of my body
feels completely relaxed. The lower half of my
body feels so relaxed and heavy, I feel as though
I don't have energy enough to move any of its
parts. I don't feel like moving any of its
parts... All I feel like doing is going deeper and
deeper into relaxation...."

"Now I am aware that the lower half of my body
feels so much heavier than the upper half. This is
because the lower half is so much more relaxed.
The relaxation and heaviness of the lower half of
my body is creating a longing for the upper half to
feel just as relaxed...That feeling of heaviness is
now moving into my abdominal regions and chest
area...My stomach feels heavy, and my chest feels
heavy. I am beginning to feel relaxed and heavy
all over...My shoulders are relaxed. My arms are
relaxed. My head is relaxed....I have a growing
feeling of just...letting go...No anxieties, no
worries, no tensions, and no feelings associated

with bodily function. I am so tired, my body feels
so heavy, I am so relaxed, I have no desire or
energy to make any movements that require conscious
effort.   I   don't   feel   like   making   any
movements...All I feel like doing is enjoying this
comfortable feeling of complete relaxation...(end)"
==

        c. Mental conditioning

While in your self-induced state of hypnosis, your
mind is prepared for mental conditioning through
self-suggestion. Use the instructions given below.
==

INSTRUCTIONS: SELF-SUGGESTIONS

"Now that my body is fully relaxed, my mind is
fully free. At this moment I choose to direct this
freedom toward my awareness of my life. This
awareness is the primary source of my existence. I
have one of the most beautiful gifts of nature,
life on earth. By accepting this life, I also
accept responsibility for it, how it is lived, and
what is accomplished in its span.

I will take and maintain control of my life; master
my fate, and be responsible for the condition of my
mental and physical health.   I will always be
logical in my thinking and constructive in my
actions.   I   will assess each aspect of my life,
prepare a plan of mastery according to the time and
energy I have available, and set realistic goals
accordingly.   I will follow my plan, challenge my
obstacles, and complete my goals".

==

Practice mental conditioning at least once per
week, until you have completed all the goals of
your PSM program. Feel free to make adjustments in
your   self-suggested mental conditioning   in
accordance with your progress.   If you do not go
into   an   actual hypnotic trance during   self-

-95-

induction, do not worry. Do continue with your self-suggestions for mental conditioning. A relatively deep state of relaxation will serve you just as well. The more you practice, however, the better you will be able to reach your desired state.

After each session of mental conditioning, and before moving around, verbally say to yourself, "I am awake." Then slap your hands together and say, "I am alert." This will assure you that you return to your regular state of alertness. Through mental conditioning you will develop a mental "set" for successful completion of your **PSM** program.

CHAPTER 6.

Organization and Time-energy Assessment

TIME AND ENERGY

In our age of convenience, sophistication, ever-growing urbanization, and inflation, getting through a day in the life of modern man is like trying to keep pace with a treadmill that never stops. The demands of living are becoming greater and stronger, and we are afraid to rest for fear of falling behind, or being swept under. Though we have developed numerous shortcuts, and are getting around as fast as we can, there still doesn't seem to be enough time. Go, go, go, and rush, rush, rush seems to be our daily diet.

When the requirements of day-to-day living become exceptionally overwhelming to people for prolonged periods of time, they begin to feel crushed. Their energy, interests, and motivation level begin to decline, gradually leading to feelings of estrangement. Such a state of affairs are beginning signs of burnout and depression.

At the onset of burnout or depression, when something is demanding energy and time that we just do not have, we might begin to feel, "what's the use, how can I take on everything at once." Whether or not our energy is depleted, we begin to feel, move, and act as though it were. Our body's resistance is lowered, making us prone to illness.

In most cases, feelings of burnout, depression, and being overwhelmed are avoidable and unnecessary. Our body has a reasonable tolerance for overwork, but we do not have to live our lives on the brink of physical and mental exhaustion. Many of us take life for granted, oblivious to the fact that we can run out of energy. We never know that we are burnt out until one day we just cannot get going.

In a sense, our body is like an automobile. We use it to carry us through our journeys in life. Like an automobile, when we want to use it to reach a certain destination, we must know how much fuel it takes and be realistic as to how much we have available. If we are in a car, driving north from California and have only enough fuel to get to Oregon, why set our sights for Canada? Those of us who would "take off for Canada" with no awareness of how much fuel we had would not only find ourselves out of fuel, but desolate.

There are some people who take off on journeys and are not only ignorant of their fuel supply, but also lack a sense of course and direction. Their disposition in operating their transportation source is to just go. Where they are going and why seem to make little or no difference. They see every mile as the last and their destination is where they end up.

People going through life in this manner are showing definite signs of a defeatist attitude, and an unwillingness to assume responsibility. Such an attitude is not innate, rather, it is an end result of their lifelong obstinacy and inflexibility. Throughout life, "their way" was the only way they have known to accomplish or resolve anything. For them, there are only two colors and two numbers; black and white, and zero and ten, there are no grays or numbers in between. Anything that does not fit, they make it fit. When "square pegs won't

go into round holes", they go to the tool chest and
get out the file and hammer, or a knife to carve
the edges. As a child they seem to have never
given up their egocentric and persevering nature.
Sooner or later (more often later) in life they
learn that the world does not revolve around them.
However, in many cases by the time they have
reached this rude awakening, they have become
unchangeable, burned out, "wills of iron".

Rather than admitting their difficulty and consider
seeking or listening to the advice of others, they
find it easier to just give up. When they reach
this futilistic state, they begin to look for
excuses and blame others for their feelings of
defeat and failure, as opposed to considering
change. They find passive-agressive revenge
through self-destruction by way of their "I'm not
responsible" attitude. "Come what may ", is their
slogan, "I'm in the hands of fate." Their
rationale, "I've tried everything. Nothing has,
can, or will work for me".

The awareness that such people have missed out on,
is that there is more to "trying" than just trying
per se; or how hard and how much you try. Of equal
importance is what you try (does it fit for you),
being well organized and having a plan before
exerting your efforts. If the plan you have does
not work, you must be flexible and choose alternate
plans. Initial assessments and frequent evaluations are also essential.

In our approach to life we usually fall into one of
three groups: "planners", "plan-as-you-goers", and
"just-goers".

Just-goers are the wheel spinners in life. They
make grand and impressive starts, but are usually
the first to poop out. They have fast beginnings
but quick ends. Such people are more impulsive,
and seldom think of planning. When they do , it is
often after they have exhausted all trial-and-error
approaches. However, at this point they usually

have little or no energy left and complain that planning is too difficult or just not worthwhile. Eventualy, they become the I'm-not-responsible-persons described earlier.

The **plan-as-you-goers** are crisis-oriented people who feel they never need to look ahead or make a complete plan. They feel confident that they can always adjust on the spot and handle all situations as they pop up. Planning, therefore, is generally seen as a waste of time. These folks seldom worry unless situations are presented at a crisis level. When this occurs, they become very excited and pool all their energy, time and efforts into on-the-spot decision-making. They never resolve the problem completely, but settle it temporarily, preserving their energy and readiness to deal with the next crisis.

Their lives are run on a "rob Peter to pay Paul", method, and they apply oil only to doors that make the loudest squeaks. For some people this method works well and for long periods of time. However, usually they are operating on borrowed time, and it catches up with them sooner or later. There comes a time when Peter begins to feel shortchanged, and his demands become equal to those of Paul; or when more doors begin to squeak than they have oil to silence. At this stage they find themselves subjected to multiple crises with energy enough for only one. Such a state of affairs makes them prime subjects for exhaustion and burnout.

Planners on the other hand, realize the advantages in the organization and assessment of available time and energy, before taking on projects and exerting their efforts. They tend to be more practical in their endeavors. They don't start fast but they last longer, tend to be less frustrated, and encounter fewer crises. When a problem does occur, there is less chance that more than one will occur at the same time. Planners are more detailed and seldom skip steps. They are more in charge of their lives and better able to master

the demands of day-to-day living without feeling
constrained or overwhelmed by it all. They are
aware of where they are going, what they are doing,
how much time and energy they are using, and how
much of the same they have available. Such
awareness facilitates much more realistic goal-
setting and more effectiveness in management and
control of their lives.

TIME AND STRESS MANAGEMENT SURVEYS, I AND II

The **Time and Stress Management Survey (T-SMS)** is an
assessment device I have devised to provide an
overview of each aspect of life and how we are
organized as to the time and energy we have
available. Each aspect is placed in one of five
categories: privacy, home, career or career
pursuits, social interaction, and miscellaneous.
These categories are defined in the instructions
for using the survey. The **T-SMS** is designed for
planners, or those who would like to become
planners. Those of you who are diehard just-goers
or plan-as-you-goers will probably skip the survey
or complete only parts of it. Whichever is your
plight, those who do complete the survey will find
it beneficial in completing the overall **PSM**
program.

Without a doubt, the organization of work is at
times more laborious than the work itself.
However, as any administrator or manager would
confess, most effort without organization is self-
defeating; more often than not, wasted, or in
general nonproductive. Such may be the case for
completing the T-SMS.

As a class project in psychology courses I teach, I
frequently require my students to administer
fifteen to twenty T-SMS's in order to gain
experience in the applied use of surveys. In their
reports, many of the students indicated that their
subjects (persons to whom they rendered the survey)
at first found the surveys laborious and time-
consuming. However, upon completion of the survey,

their subjects reported that they felt a great
sense of accomplishment. They gained insight, and
most of all, concern for whether they were spending
their time and energy according to their
priorities. Many were able to locate sources of
stress in how they spent their time; others became
conscientious of their lack of organization and
need for planning.

The **T-SMS** is based on a twenty-four hour day (from
12 a.m. one day to 12 a.m. the next) and a seven-
day week; its purpose is to assess the time and
energy we have available, and how it is spent in a
one hundred sixty-eight hour week. Two forms are
provided, T-SMS I and T-SMS II.

T-SMS I should be filled out according to how you
(actual or estimated) spend your time and energy at
present. **T-SMS II** is provided to indicate what
adjustments you would make according to how you
would like to spend your time and energy if you had
a choice. Before you begin filling out your
survey(s), review the example and instructions
given below:

EXAMPLE: Monday

1 PRIVACY

(a). Sleep:
   - Woke up at 7 a.m. (12 a.m. to 7 a.m.) = 7 hours
   - Went or plan to go to bed at 11 p.m.
    (11 p.m. to 12 a.m) = 1 hr.
       Total hours sleep for Monday: = 8 hours

(b). Rest/Relaxation:
   - Read for a half hour during
    lunch break = 0.5 hours
   - Watched T.V. for 1-1/2 hours
    after supper = 1.5 hr.
       Total Rest/Relaxation = 2 hr

(c). **Exercise:** Did one half hour of stretching
   exercises and yoga after returning home

from work   = 0.5 hr

Did one half hour of stretching exercises and
yoga before going to bed.   = 0.5 hr
          Total Exercise for Monday: = 1 hr

2. HOME
(a). With spouse and/or lover:
    - Spent one half hour at breakfast
      together   = 0.5 hr
    - Spent one half hour at supper
      together   = 0.5 hr
    - Had one hour of verbal and/or
      physical interaction before
      going to sleep   = 1 hr
              Total time spent with
              spouse or lover   = 2 hours

(b). With others in the home
    - Spent one half hour with kids
      when I came in from work   = 0.5 hr
    - Spent one half hour playing with kids
      before sending them to bed   = 0.5 hr
              Total time spent with others
              in the home   = 1 hr
(c). Doing household chores:
    - Spent one half hour cleaning the
      kitchen after supper   = 0.5 hr
              Total time spent doing
              household chores   = 0.5 hr

3. CAREER
   Arrived at work at 8:30 am. had an
   hour lunch, left at 5:30   = 8 hrs
              Total time spent on career on
              Monday   = 8 hrs

4. SOCIAL INTERACTION
   Didn't spend any time interacting socially
   today   = 0 hr
              Total time spent at social
              interacting Monday   = 0 hr

5. MISCELLANEOUS

```
Left home for work at 7:45 a.m., arrived
at work at 8:30 a. m.                          = 45 min


Left work at 5:30 p.m., arrived home at
6:15  p.m.                                     = 45 min
            Total hours spent commuting
            (misc.) for Monday.                = 1.5 hr
```

Total time and energy for Monday:
```
    Privacy  (a + b + c)                       = 11.0 hrs
    Home     (a + b + c)                       =  3.5
    Career                                     =  8.0
    Social  Interacting                        =  0.
    Miscellaneous                              =  1.5
                                 TOTAL         = 24.0 hrs
```

The above figures for Monday would appear as follows on your **T-SMS I**:

	PRIVACY			HOME			CAREER	SOCIAL INT.	MISC.	Totals
	a	b	c	a	b	c				
Monday	8	2	1	2	1	.5	8	0	1.5	24 hrs.
	a+b+c= 11			a+b+c= 3.5						
Tuesd~~ay~~	~~a+b+~~c=			a+~~b~~						

INSTRUCTIONS:

(1) Similar estimates should be made and recorded
on your **T-SMS I** for each day of the week until the
survey is complete.

(2) While filling out the survey, keep in mind that
your totals for each day should always equal 24
hours; this is more important than having an exact
estimate of how you spend your time.   Use a pencil
to complete your survey(s) should you have to make
adjustments.

(3) When each 24-hour day is accounted for, it
should equal a 168 hour week.   In the space

provided (Levels of Stress), on a scale of 1 through 10, very stressed (10-9-8-7-6-5-4-3-2-1) to not stresssed, <u>rank</u> the level of stress you feel due to a particular difficulty, or resulting from too much or too little time and energy spent in each category.

(4) When you have completed the **T-SMS I**, proceed to complete the **T-SMS II**.

(5) **T-SMS II** is to be completed in a manner similar to **T-SMS I**. The difference will be that (a) the figures you record should be based on how much time and energy you **would like** to spend in a 24-hour day for each category, **if you had a choice;** and, (b) you **should not** record figures in the space provided for ranking (Levels of Stress) for each category until instructed to do so in later chapters of the book, where you will set goals to meet your likes and choices.
===

TIME AND STRESS MANAGEMENT SURVEY (T-SMS I)

Instructions:

A. Based on a 24-hour day, record the number of hours (estimated or actual) spent in each of the categories listed below.

1. **PRIVACY**
a. Sleep
b. Rest/Relaxation
c. Exercise

2. **HOME**
a. With spouse and/or lover
b. With others in the home
c. Doing household chores

3. **CAREER/CAREER PURSUITS** (includes work and related education)

4. **SOCIAL INTERACTING** (time spent outside of the home with friends, associates, and relatives)

5. **MISCELLANEOUS** (travel, commute, errands, etc.)

	PRIVACY			HOME			CAREER	SOCIAL INT.	MISC.	Totals
	a	b	c	a	b	c				
Monday	a+b+c=			a+b+c=						24 hrs.
Tuesday	a+b+c=			a+b+c=						24 hrs.
Wednesday	a+b+c=			a+b+c=						24 hrs.
Thrusday	a+b+c=			a+b+c=						24 hrs.
Friday	a+b+c=			a+b+c=						24 hrs.
Saturday	a+b+c=			a+b+c=						24 hrs.
Sunday	a+b+c=			a+b+c=						24 hrs.
Totals	a+b+c=			a+b+c=						168 hrs.
Levels of Stress	a+b+c÷3=			a+b+c÷3=						

B. In the space provided below the totals of each category, rank the level of stress you feel, using a scale of one to ten, very stressed (10-9-8-7-6-5-4-3-2-1) to not stresed, related to each category.

TIME AND STRESS MANAGEMENT SURVEY (T-SMS II)

Instructions:

A. Based on a 24 hour day, record the estimated amount of time you feel would be ideal to meet the needs and demands of each category with minimal stress.

1. PRIVACY
a. Sleep
b. Rest/Relaxation
c. Exercise

2. HOME
a. With spouse and/or lover
b. With others in the home
c. Doing household chores

3. CAREER/CAREER PURSUITS
   (includes work and related education)

4. SOCIAL INTERACTING
(Time spent outside of the home with friends, associates, and relatives)

5. MISCELLANEOUS (travel, commute, errands, etc.)

	PRIVACY			HOME			CAREER	SOCIAL INT.	MISC.	Totals
	a	b	c	a	b	c				
Monday	a+b+c=			a+b+c=						24 hrs.
Tuesday	a+b+c=			a+b+c=						24 hrs.
Wednesday	a+b+c=			a+b+c=						24 hrs.
Thrusday	a+b+c=			a+b+c=						24 hrs.
Friday	a+b+c=			a+b+c=						24 hrs.
Saturday	a+b+c=			a+b+c=						24 hrs.
Sunday	a+b+c=			a+b+c=						24 hrs.
Totals	a+b+c=			a+b+c=						168 hrs.
Levels of Stress	a+b+c÷3=			a+b+c÷3=						

B. Until further instructed, do not fill in the space provided for the level of stress.

===

The awareness created by filling out these charts places us in a better position to take control of our lives. It also allows us to set more realistic goals. In particular, for purposes of a **Personalized Stress Management** it allows us to pinpoint the sources of time and energy strain in our lives, and make realistic adjustments.

One of the many reasons people are unable to relieve their own depression or recover from burnout is that they are unable to locate the **source** of strain. They feel a need to lash or act out, but they have no logical direction. This results in their taking their frustration out on themselves through self-pity, ailments, etc.; or the displacement of anger and aggression directed toward their peers and loved ones (hence the classic example of being angry at your boss and coming home and kicking the dog).

The **Time and Stress Management Survey** provides a general reference for the chapters that follow. Upon its completion, we are prepared to identify and work with our sources of stress in an organized manner, and in accordance with the limits of time and energy we have available. The chapters that follow are in workbook form in order to provide individualized participation in assessing and developing a **PSM** program.

Before proceeding, a word of caution is offered in regards to the Goal Assessment sections of your program development, and should be considered in your goal-setting decisions. That is, these assessments are based on your own self-reports, which limits their validity to how reliable **you** feel the results are based on the answers **you** give at the time of completing the questionnaires. By design, however, this contributes to the individualized nature of the assessments, and eliminates the need for established norms.

CHAPTER 7.

Privacy: (a) Sleep
(b) Rest & Relaxation
(c) Exercise

PRIVACY consists of the special and intimate time we spend with ourselves for the purpose of mental and physical rejuvenation of energy exerted throughout the day, and our conditioning and preparation for the next. It is that personal space we need to digest the experiences of the day and prepare our menu and its ingredients for the next. Through privacy, we gain our sense of order and preparation which determines the mode of inspiration of how our day will begin and end.

Though mental-conditioning is listed as number one in the **PSM** program, it should take place during **privacy**, as does sleep, rest, and relaxation, and exercise.

==
(a). Sleep
==

GOAL ASSESSMENT:

Using the space provided, on a scale of one to five, definite yes (5-4-3-2-1) to definitely no, rate yourself on the following questions:

1. I seldom feel rested when I awake. _____

2. I have pleasant dreams. _____

3. I think better when I get enough
   sleep. _____

4. Not enough sleep effects my mood. _____

5. I love sleep. _____

6. I constantly feel I need naps when
   I don't get enough sleep. _____

7. I tire easily. _____

8. I need stimulants to keep me going
   throughout the day. _____

9. Frequently people tell me I look
   tired. _____

10. I feel better about myself when I
    get enough sleep. _____

                              TOTAL: _____

==

Interpretation of Answers:

Multiply the total score by 2 to get a percentage
score.

Your total score _____ X2 = _____ %

Your percentage score indicates how important sleep
is to your ability to cope with stress.

     80 - 100%   Extremely important

     70 - 80%   Very important

     60 - 70%   Moderately important

  Below   50%   Not important

Refer to your **Time Management Survey II** (page 107). In the subcategory sleep (under PRIVACY) what was your total figure for the week indicating the amount of sleep you would like (need) to feel rested if you had a choice.

_____

Refer to your weekly totals (**Sleep**) in your **Time Management Survey I** (page 106). How much sleep do you actually get per week?

_____

Subtract: _____

(1)   If the amount of sleep you are getting is equal to the amount of sleep you feel you need, you do not need to set goals for sleep.

(2)   If the amount of sleep you are getting is more than the amount of sleep you need to feel rested throughout the day, then you should cut down on the number of hours you sleep and set goals for making better use of this time.

(3)   If the amount of sleep you are getting is less than you need, you should set goals for getting an amount that will enable you to feel rested throughout the day.

==

DECISION AND PLANNING:

1. I should set sleep goals for myself?

    Yes _____ No _____

2. If yes, my sleep goals are: _____

_____

3. In order, what are the specific steps I will take to reach my goal?

     (a) _____

     (b) _____

     (c) _____

4. The obstacles (personal and otherwise) that stand in the way of obtaining my goals are:

     (a) _____

     (b) _____

     (c) _____

5. I plan to reduce these obstacles by:

     (a) _____

     (b) _____

     (c) _____

6. Here is a list of people who can help me with my goals and how:

PERSON	HOW
(a) _____	_____
(b) _____	_____
(c) _____	_____
(d) _____	_____

7. I plan to dicuss my sleep goals with the above named persons.   Yes _____   No _____

==

PLAN IMPLEMENTATION AND COMMITMENT:

1. The exact date and time I will commit myself to execute my plan is:

   Date _____   Time _____

2. The persons who will be a witness to my commitment are:

   (a) _____

   (b) _____

3. The date I can reliably evaluate whether my plan is working is: Date _____ 19___

==

COMMITMENT CONTRACT

I_____ on this _____day of _____19____ do commit myself to the above-described plan that is designed to reduce the level of stress I feel in relation to **sleep**. I will evaluate my plan on time. If my plan is not working, I will make adjustments as they are needed, or choose an alternate plan.

Signature _____Date _____19___

Witnessed by: _____Date _____19___

_____Date _____19___

==

EVALUATION: Date _____19___

1. Refer to **T-SMS II**, (page 107).   In the   space
    provided, record the current (to date) level of
    stress you feel for the category of **sleep**.

2. Compare the level of stress recorded in
    T-SMS I to that recorded in **T-SMS II**,
    and register the information below:

                T-SMS I level of stress   _____

                T-SMS II level of stress   _____

        Decrease or increase level of
        stress   Subtract   _____

3. Based on the decrease or increase in your level
    of stress, is your plan working? Yes__ No___

4. If no, what is interfering with your plan?

    a. _____

    b. _____

5. Do you need adjustment in your plan? Yes__ No__

6. If yes, what adjustments can be made?

    a. _____

    b. _____

7. Do you need another plan?   Yes___   No ____

8. If yes, in order of specific steps, what is
   your alternative plan(s)?

    a. _____

    b. _____

```
==========================================================
```
(b). Rest and Relaxation
```
==========================================================
```

GOAL ASSESSMENT:

Using the space provided, on a scale of one to
five, definitely no (5-4-3-2-1) definitely yes,
rate yourself on the following statements:

1. Vacations are important to me. _____

2. I can turn off the pressures of
   the day easily. _____

3. When working, I take a break when
   I get tired or feel tension. _____

4. I know what relaxes me most. _____

5. I take time out for myself. _____

6. I like to work under pressure. _____

7. I feel good instead of guilty
   when I take time to do nothing
   but relax. _____

8. It is easy for me to allow myself
   to relax. _____

9. I plan relaxation activities. _____

10. I take time out for myself
    just to do nothing. _____

                    TOTAL   _____

```
==========================================================
```

Calculations: Multiply your total score by 2 to
get a percentage score.

Your total score _____ X2 = _____ %

Your percentage score is indicative of your need
for settings goals for rest and relaxation.

    80 - 100%   Very strong need

    70 - 80%   Strong need

    60 - 70%   Relatively strong need

    50 - 60%   Medium need

Under 50%   You are probably getting the
                       rest and relaxation you need.

Referring to your **T-SMS II,** how
much rest and relaxation do you feel
you need during the week? _____

Referring to your **T-SMS I,** how
much rest and relaxation do you actually
get during the week? _____

I should increase/decrease rest and
relaxation time by:
                   SUBTRACT _____

==

DECISION <u>AND</u> <u>PLANNING</u>:

1. I should set rest and relaxation goals for
myself?

Yes _____   No _____

2. If yes, my rest and relaxation goals are:

_____

3. In order, the specific steps I will take to reach my goal are:

(a) _____

(b) _____

(c) _____

(d) _____

4. The obstacles (personal and otherwise) that stand in the way of obtaining my goals are:

(a) _____

(b) _____

(c) _____

5. I plan to reduce these obstacles by:

(a) _____

(b) _____

(c) _____

(d) _____

6. Here is a list of the people who can help me with my goals and how:

(a) _____

(b) _____

(c) _____

7. I plan to discuss my rest and relaxation goals with the above persons. Yes_____ No_____

==

PLAN IMPLEMENTATION AND COMMITMENT

1. The exact date and time I will commit myself to execute my plan is:

Date _____ Time _____

2. The persons who will be a witness to my commitment are:

a. _____

b. _____

3. The date I can reliably evaluate whether my plan is working is: Date_____19__

===

COMMITMENT CONTRACT

I_____ on   this _____day   of
_____19 ____ do commit myself to the   above-
described   plan that is designed   to reduce   the
level   of   stress I feel in relation to **rest   and
relaxation**. I will evaluate my plan on time.   If
my plan is not working, I will make adjustments as
they are needed, or choose an alternate plan.

Signature _____Date _____19__

Witnessed by: _____Date _____19__

_____Date _____19__

<u>EVALUATION</u>   Date _____ 19__

1.   Refer to **T-SMS II**, (page 107).   In the space
     provided, record the current (to date) level of
     stress you feel for the category of **rest and
     relaxation**

2.   Compare the level of stress recorded in
     T-SMS I to that recorded in **T-SMS II**,
     and register the information below:

             T-SMS I level of stress   _____

             T-SMS II level of stress   _____

          Decrease or increase in level of
          stress   Subtract   _____

3. Based on the decrease or increase in your level
of stress, is your plan working?   Yes___   No___

4. If no, what is interfering with your plan?

a. _____

b. _____

5. Do you need adjustments in your plan? Yes__ No__

6. If yes, what adjustments can be made?

a. _____

b. _____

7. Do you need another plan?   Yes___   No____

8. If yes, in order of specific steps, what is your
alternative plans(s)?

a. _____

b. _____

==
(c). Exercise
==

GOAL ASSESSMENT

Using the space provided, on a scale of one to
five, definitely no (5-4-3-2-1) to definitely yes,
rate yourself on the following questions:

1. Do you have a regular exercise
    program?   _____

2. Do you get the amount of exercise
    you need?   _____

3. Do you feel an urge to exercise
    after sitting for long periods
    of time?   _____

4. Has your doctor discouraged you
    from having an exercise program? _____

5. Do you often walk up stairs
    rather than take an elevator?   _____

6. Do you exercise to relieve
    tension?   _____

7. Does exercise appeal to you?   _____

8. Would you rather participate in sports
    events than be a spectator?   _____

9. Do you feel physically fit?   _____

10. Do you feel restless when
    you don't exercise?   _____

                              TOTAL   _____

==
Calculations: Multiply your total score by 2 to
get a percentage score.

Your total score _____ X2 _____ %

Your percentage score is indicative of your need to set up an exercise program for yourself. Scores of 50% and higher indicate that you are missing out on a very important aspect of coping with stress. Please re-read the section on exercise in Chapter 4 for reiteration of the importance of exercise in coping with stress.

80 to 100%   Very strong need

70 to 80%   Strong need

60 to 70%   Relatively strong need

50 to 60%   Moderately strong need

Below 50%   You are probably getting the exercise you need.

If you need an exercise program, then definite goals should be set. For ideas in setting up your goals, circle the letter that indicates your exercise and time preference.

What time would you prefer to exercise?

a. In the morning, fresh out of bed.

b. During your lunch hour

c. After work

d. Before bed

e. Other _____

What type of exercise do you prefer?

    a. Calisthenics

    b. Jogging

    c. Yoga (bend and stretch exercises)

    d. Competitve sports

    e. Combinations of _____

    f. Other _____

Instructions for a very simple, but effective exercise program are as follows:

1. Visit your neighborhood athletic equipment store and purchase the following:

    a. Sweat suit
    b. Running shoes
    c. Jump rope

2. On days you have to work, before going to bed, do the following:

    a. Spend 10 to 15 minutes practicing a few of your favored stretch and posture exercises described in Chapter Four.

    b. Set your alarm <u>15</u> minutes earlier than usual.

    c. Lay out your sweat suit and jump rope in a handy place near the bed.

3. When the alarm goes off the following morning, get out of bed, put on your sweat suit, take your jump rope, go to an appropriate place in the house, and do <u>15</u> minutes of jumping rope. Do this until you have mastered jumping rope 50 times without fault. Then move to <u>20</u> minutes of jumping rope

without fault 100 times.

4. On days you do not have to work, take a walk to the park or a convenient track field dressed in your running shoes and sweat suit and jog one or two laps. Try to increase a lap each day you go.

If you are a beginner, please be aware of the following precautions before you set up your exercise program:

(1) Plan a tentative fitness program and be sure it is appropriate for your age and ability.

(2) If you are over 35 or have a known physical condition, get a medical clearance first.

(3) Avoid overexertion. Be sure you have the energy for the exercise you begin.

==

DECISION PLANNING:

1. I should set exercise goals for myself?

Yes _____   No _____

2. If yes, my exercise goals are: _____

_____

_____

3. In order, the specific steps I will take to achieve my goals are:

(a) _____

(b) _____

(c) _____

4. The obstacles (personal and otherwise) that stand in the way of obtaining my goals are:

(a) _____

(b) _____

(c) _____

(d) _____

5. I plan to reduce these obstacles by:

(a) _____

(b) _____

(c) _____

(d) _____

6. Here is a list of the people who can help me with my goals and how:

PERSON   HOW

(a) _____   _____

(b) _____   _____

(c) _____   _____

(d) _____   _____

7. I plan to discuss my exercise goals with the above-named persons.

Yes _____   No _____

PLAN AND IMPLEMENTATION AND COMMITMENT:

1. The exact date and time I will commit myself to exercise my plan is:

Date _____   Time _____

2. The persons who will be a witness to my commitment are:

a. _____

b. _____

3. The date I can reliably evaluate whether my plan is working is: Date _____19__

COMMITMENT CONTRACT

I_____ on this _____day of _____ 19 ___ do commit myself to the above-described plan that is designed to reduce the level of stress I feel in relation to **exercise**. I will evaluate my plan on time. If my plan is not working, I will make adjustments as they are needed, or choose an alternate plan.

Signature _____Date _____19__

Witnessed by: _____Date _____19__

_____Date _____19__

<u>EVALUATION</u>   Date _____19__

1. Refer to **T-SMS II**, (page 107).   In the   space
    provided, record the current (to date) level of
    stress you feel for the category of **exercise**.

2. Compare the level of stress recorded in **T-SMSI**
    to   that   recorded in **T-SMS II**, and   register
    the information below:

              T-SMS I level of stress   _____

              T-SMS II level of stress   _____

         Decrease or increase in level of
         stress   Subtract _____

3. Based on the decrease or increase in your level
of stress, is your plan working? Yes____ No____

4. If no, what is interfering with your plan?

a. _____

b. _____

5. Do you need adjustments in your plan? Yes__ No__

6. If yes, what adjustments can be made?

a. _____

b. _____

7. Do you need another plan? Yes____   No____

8. If yes, in order of specific steps, what is your
aternative plans(s)?

a. _____

b. _____

CHAPTER 8.

Home: (a) With Spouse and or Lover
(b) With Others in the Home
(c) Doing Household Chores

HOME is our primary support system. It is where our most intimate sharing takes place. The home aspect of our lives consists of the time we spend:

1. Interacting with our most intimate loved one, spouse, or lover.

2. Interacting with others in the home, children or roommates.

3. Doing daily or weekly household chores.

==
(a). Spouse and/or Lover
==

GOAL ASSESSMENT:

Using the space provided, answer True or False to the following statements:

1. My relationship fulfills my   _____
   expectations.

2. I am satisfied with the amount of   _____

time I spend with my partner.

3. There is nothing I dislike about
   my partner.   _____

4. My partner is not satisfied with the
   amount of one-to-one quality time I   _____
   spend with him/her.

5. It's hard for my partner and me to
   talk when we have a disagreement.   _____

6. My relationship causes me stress.   _____

7. I feel insecure in my relationship.   _____

8. I avoid spending time with my
   partner.   _____

9. There is lots of spark in my
   relationship.   _____

10. I catch myself doing or creating
    other things to do in place of
    spending time on an intimate level
    with my partner.   _____

11. Sexual attraction is at a high level
    of intensity in my relationship.   _____

12. I feel close to my partner.   _____

13. I find it difficult to confide
    in my partner.   _____

14. I have good communication with my
    partner.   _____

15. I look forward to being with my
    partner after being separated   _____
    during the day.

16. I feel there is an unresolved
    conflict in my relationship.   _____

17. I love my partner. _____

18. I feel that my partner tries to
consume too much of my time. _____

19. There is something missing in my
relationship. _____

20. My partner is responsible and
reliable. _____

==

Interpretation of answers:

In nonstressful relationships,

The preferable answer for numbers 1,2,3,9,11,12,
14, 15, 17, and 20 is <u>True</u>.

The preferable answer for numbers 4, 5, 6, 7, 8,
10, 13, 16, 18, and 19 is <u>False</u>.

If fifteen or more of your answers correspond to
the above, you would appear to have a non-stressful
relationship. If less than ten correspond, perhaps
you should set goals to improve your relationship.

For ideas about what areas need improvement in your
relationship, study the list below. Circle the
letters that indicate difficulty in your
relationship and give the most significant
reason(s) you feel a difficulty exists. Be
specific.

<u>REASON</u>

a. Finance _____

b. Sex _____

c. Personal Habits _____

d. Relatives _____

e. Communication _____

f. Physical Appearance _____

g. Kids _____

h. No kids _____

i. Boredom _____

j. Personality
    Conflict _____

k. Lack of
    Consideration _____

l. Other _____ _____

    _____

==

DECISION AND PLANNING:

1. I should set relationship goals?

   Yes _____ No _____

2. If yes, my relation goals are: _____

_____

3. In order, what are the specific steps I will
    take to reach my goal?

        (a) _____

        (b) _____

        (c) _____

        (d) _____

4. The obstacles (personal and otherwise) that stand in the way of obtaining my goal are:

(a) _____

(b) _____

(c) _____

(d) _____

5. I plan to reduce these obstacles by:

(a) _____

(b) _____

(c) _____

(d) _____

6. Here is a list of persons who can help me with my goals and how:

PERSON   HOW

(a) _____   _____

(b) _____   _____

(c) _____   _____

(d) _____   _____

7. I plan to dicuss my relationship goals with the above named persons.

Yes _____   No _____

===

PLAN IMPLEMENTATION AND COMMITMENT:

1. The exact date and time I will commit
   myself to execute my plan is:

   Date _____   Time _____

2. Who will be a witness to my commitment?

   (a) _____

   (b) _____

3. The date I can reliably evaluate whether my plan
   is working is: Date _____19__

COMMITMENT CONTRACT

I _____on this _____day
of _____19__ do commit myself to the above
described plan that is designed to reduce the level
of stress I feel in regards to my **relationship**.   I
will evaluate my plan on time.   If my plan is not
working, I will make adjustments as they are
needed, or choose an alternate plan.

Signature_____Date_____19__

Witnessed by: _____Date_____19__

_____Date_____19__

EVALUATION: Date_____19__

1. Refer to **T-SMS II** (page 107). In the space provided, record the current (to date) level of stress you feel for the subcategory of **spouse and/or lover**.

2. Compare the level of stress recorded in **T-SMS I** to that recorded in **T-SMS II**, and register the information below.

    T-SMS I level of stress   _____

    T-SMS II level of stress   _____

    Decrease or increase in level of
    stress   Subtract _____

3. Based on the decrease or increase in your level of stress, is your plan working? Yes__ No__

4. If no, what is interfering with your plan?

    a. _____

    b. _____

5. Do you need adjustment in your plan? Yes__ No__

6. If yes, what adjustments can be made?

    a. _____

    b. _____

7. Do you need another plan? Yes____   No____

8. If yes, in order of specific steps, what is your alternative plan(s)?

    a. _____

    b. _____

==
(b) Others in the Home
==

GOAL ASSESSMENT:

Using the space provided, answer True or False to
the following statements:

1. Others in the home annoy me
    frequently.   _____

2. I have enough time to spend with
    others in the home.   _____

3. Others in the home put too many
    demands on me.   _____

4. I enjoy others in the home who live
    with me.   _____

5. I feel that others in the home create _____
    more responsibility than I want
    to handle.

6. I seldom have to avoid spending time _____
    with others in the home.

7. Sometimes I feel there are too many
    people living with me.   _____

8. Spending time with others in the home
    often releases tension for me.   _____

9. It's not my responsibility to spend
    time with others in the home.   _____

10. I find it easy to find my own space _____
    when I don't want to be around
    others in the home.

==

Interpretation of answers:

In nonstressful home relationships,

The preferable answer for the odd numbers is
False.

The preferable answer for the even numbers is
True.

If seven or more of your answers correspond to the
above, you would appear not to have stress that is
related to others in the home. Having five or
fewer answers that correspond is indicative of
difficulty in this area that causes stress. Stress
in this area is usually caused by feelings of
pressure and demands for time that is not available
when requested. Examples of goals for minimizing
stress in this area are:
----

1. Confronting the issue by getting together,
discussing the problem and expectations, and brain-
storming suggestions.

2. Planning when you can spend time with others in
the home without conflicting with your need for
space or rest.

3. Suggesting possible trade-offs and means of
cooperation whereby you would also benefit from any
extra time you spend with others in the home.
==

DECISION AND PLANNING:

1. I should set goals for reducing stress related to
   others in the home.

Yes _____   No _____

2. If yes, my goals are:

_____

3. In order, the specific steps I will take to reach my goal are:

(a) _____

(b) _____

(c) _____

4. The obstacles (personal and otherwise) that stand in the way of obtaining my goal are:

(a) _____

(b) _____

(c) _____

5. I plan to reduce these obstacles by:

(a) _____

(b) _____

(c) _____

6. Here is a list of the people who can help me with my goals and how:

(a) _____

(b) _____

(c) _____

(d) _____

7. I plan to discuss my goals for others in the home. Yes _____ No _____

===

PLAN IMPLENTATION AND COMMITMENT

1. The exact date and time I will commit myself
    to execute my plan is:

Date _____   Time _____

2. The persons who will be a witness to my
    commitments are:

a. _____

b. _____

3. The date I can reliably evaluate whether my
plan is working is: Date_____19__

COMMITMENT CONTRACT

I _____on this _____day
of _____19__ do commit myself to the above
described plan that is designed to reduce the level
of stress I feel in regards to **others in the home**.
I will evaluate my plan on time. If my plan is not
working, I will make adjustments as they are
needed, or choose an alternate plan.

Signature_____Date_____19__

Witnessed by: _____Date_____19__

                _____Date_____19__

<u>EVALUATION</u>   Date _____ 19__

1. Refer to **T-SMS II** (page 107). In the space provided, record the current (to date) level of stress you feel for the subcategory of **others in the home**.

2. Compare the level of stress recorded in **T-SMS I** to that recorded in **T-SMS II**, and register the information below.

            T-SMS I level of stress   _____

            T-SMS II level of stress   _____

        Decrease or increase in level of
        stress   Subtract _____

3. Based on the decrease or increase in your level of stress, is your plan working? Yes___ No___

4. If no, what is interfering with your plan?

a. _____

b. _____

5. Do you need adjustments in your plan? Yes___ No___

6. If yes, what adjustments can be made?

a. _____

b. _____

7. Do you need another plan? Yes___ No___

8. If yes, in order of specific steps, what is your alternative plans(s)?

a. _____

b. _____

```
========================================================
              (c) Household Chores
========================================================
```

GOAL ASSESSMENT

Use the space provided, answer True or False to the
following statements:

1. I have too many things to do around   _____
    the house.
2. I feel that there is equal sharing of   _____
    responsibility for the household
    chores.
3. I seldom feel stuck in a gender role   _____
    insofar as household chores are
    concerned.
4. I feel the amount of work I do around   _____
    the house is well appreciated.
5. I seldom feel my work around the   _____
    house is never done.
6. No one has to tell me what needs to   _____
    be done around the house.
7. I never have enough time to finish   _____
    my chores.
8. I feel my house needs constant   _____
    cleaning.
9. If I don't get things done around   _____
    the house they just won't get done.
10. It doesn't bother me to have to
    do chores.   _____

```
========================================================
```

Interpretation of answers:

In nonstressful arrangements regarding household
chores:

The preferable answer for numbers 2,3,4,5, and 6 is
True.

The preferable answer for numbers 1,7,8,9, and 10
is False.

If seven or more of your answers correspond to the above, it would appear you do not have stress that is related to household chores. Having five or fewer answers that correspond is indicative of the need for better organization and communication in getting household chores done. Example of goals for minimizing stress in this area are:

----

1. Discuss expectations of responsibility for chores with your spouse/lover and others in the home.

2. Keep a reference list of chores that need to be done and the people who have agreed to do them.

3. Plan your time for chores. Sort out the ones that must be done daily, and those that can be left until weekends without causing a problem.

===

DECISION PLANNING:

1. Should I set goals for better organization and communication in getting household chores done?

Yes _____   No _____

2. If yes, my goals are: _____

_____

_____

3. In order, the specific steps I will take to achieve my goal are:

(a) _____

(b) _____

(c) _____

4. The obstacles (personal and otherwise) that stand in the way of obtaining my goals are:

(a) _____

(b) _____

(c) _____

(d) _____

5. I plan to reduce these obstacles by:

(a) _____

(b) _____

(c) _____

(d) _____

6. Here is a list of people who can help me with my goals and how:

	PERSON	HOW
(a)	_____	_____
(b)	_____	_____
(c)	_____	_____
(d)	_____	_____

7. I plan to discuss my household chore goals with the above-named persons.

Yes_____   No_____

==

PLAN AND IMPLEMENTATION AND COMMITMENT:

1. The exact date and time I will commit myself to exercise my plan is:

Date _____   Time _____

2. The persons who will be a witness to my commitment are:

a. _____

b. _____

3. The date I can reliably evaluate whether my plan is working is   Date _____ 19___

COMMITMENT CONTRACT

I _____ on this _____ day of _____ 19___ do commit myself to the above described plan that is designed to reduce the level of stress I feel in regards to **household chores**. I will evaluate my plan on time.   If my plan is not working, I will make adjustments as they are needed, or choose an alternate plan.

Signature_____Date_____19__

Witnessed by: _____Date_____19__

_____Date_____19__

EVALUATION   Date _____ 19___

1. Refer to **T-SMS II** (page 107). In the space provided, record the current (to date) level of stress you feel for the subcategory of **household chores.**

2. Compare the level of stress recorded in **T-SMS I** to that recorded in **T-SMS II**, and register the information below.

              T-SMS I level of stress   _____

              T-SMS II level of stress   _____

       Decrease or increase in level of
         stress   Subtract _____

3. Based on the decrease or increase in your level of stress, is your plan working? Yes___ No___

4. If no, what is interfering with your plan?

a. _____

b. _____

5. Do you need adjustments in your plan? Yes___ No___

6. If yes, what adjustments can be made?

a. _____

b. _____

7. Do you need another plan? Yes_____   No_____

8. If yes, in order of specific steps, what is your aternative plans(s)?

a. _____

b. _____

CHAPTER 9

Career/Career
Pursuits

CAREER/CAREER PURSUITS consists of our jobs, our work, or any kind of career-related education or enrichment.

GOAL ASSESSMENT:

Using the space provided, answer True or False to the following statements:

1. I feel good about the hours I put into my career/career pursuits.   _____

2. Too often I have to sacrifice family _____ activities because of my career/career pursuits.

3. My job expects too much of me.   _____

4. My family and others see me as a workaholic.   _____

5. My work is an escape for me to get away from home.   _____

6. My work is often dull or monotomous.   _____

7. There is too much pressure on my job. _____

8. I feel my pay is adequate compensation for the work I do. _____

9. I am paid fairly compared with my fellow employees or associates. _____

10. My pay is enough to live on comfortably. _____

11. I like the way things are handled where I work. _____

12. I find some of the conditions where I work annoying. _____

13. I could do a better job at work if working conditions were better. _____

14. I am enthusiastic about my work and career. _____

15. I feel my performance at work is well up to par. _____

16. My work has adverse effects on my health. _____

17. I feel relieved the moment I get off from work. _____

18. I gain a feeling of self-esteem from my job. _____

19. I have no real respect for my supervisors. _____

20. Often I feel uptight at work without knowing the reason why. _____

===

Interpretation of answers:

The preferable answer for numbers 1,8,9,10,11,14,

15, and 18 is <u>True</u>.

The preferable answer for numbers 2,3,4,5, 6, 7, 12, 13, 16, 17, 19 and 20 is <u>False</u>.

If fifteen or more of your answers correspond to the above, you would appear to have minimal stress related to your career/career pursuits. Having ten or fewer answers that correspond suggests one or more of the following:

1. Career/job dissatisfaction or burnout.

2. Being overworked/overstressed and unaware of it.

3.   Your job serves as a displacement for managing stress in other aspects of your life.

If one or more of the above applies to you, give a specific reason why:

Reason for no. 1   _____

Reason for no. 2   _____

Reason for no. 3   _____

The reason you give should indicate the goals you set for minimizing the stress related to your career/career pursuits. Some examples of goals in this area are:

1.   Self-assessment of why you are working in your particular job or career (assessment such as, "This is the best job I can get. I can't do any better"; "I'm too lazy to change"; or "I'm too afraid to take the risk of change"). These assessments can all be challenged by setting goals, taking risk, and sticking to a commitment. Remember, there is no such thing as failure so long as you are trying. If your present employment is a stepping stone for

the next phase in your career, then you should realize that you'll be rewarded for your sacrifices; find means of tolerating the stress you are under and minimizing the resulting pressure you feel.

2. If your work is monotomous, restraining, or confining for long periods of time, substitute smoke and coffee breaks with **PSM** breaks, and practice some of the breathing, posture, and stretching exercises suggested in Chapter Four. Perhaps, if requested, your employer would consider a special room or area of privacy that would be conducive to this.

3. Make use of your support system. Share your feelings with your fellow employees or associates to get feedback as to whether it's your personal attitude or the work sitution that causes you stress.

4. If you are feeling overwhelmed by your work-load, or a particular situation, make an appointment to discuss the matter with your immediate supervisor. When you do, be sure to begin your discussion on a positive note such as asking for suggestions to help minimize your stress, rather than beginning on the defensive by unloading an accumulation of complaints.

5. If you are feeling generally burned out, put in for a vacation request. If granted, make plans to ensure that you get the rest and rejuvenation you need.
==

DECISION AND PLANNING:

1. I should set goals related to my career/career pursuits?   Yes _____   No _____

2. If yes, my career/career pursuit goals are:

_____

3. In order, what are the specific steps I will take to reach my goal?

(a) _____

(b) _____

(c) _____

4. The obstacles (personal and otherwise) that stand in the way of obtaining my goal are:

(a) _____

(b) _____

(c) _____

5. I plan to reduce these obstacles by:

(a) _____

(b) _____

(c) _____

6. Here is a list of persons who can help me with my goals and how:

PERSON   HOW

(a) _____   _____

(b) _____   _____

(c) _____   _____

7. I plan to dicuss my career/career pursuit goals with the above-named persons. Yes ___ No ____

==

PLAN IMPLEMENTATION AND COMMITMENT:

1. The exact date and time I will commit myself to execute my plan is:

   Date _____   Time _____

2. The persons who will be a witness to my commitments are?

   (a) _____

   (b) _____

3. By what date can I reliably evaluate whether my plan is working? Date _____ 19__

COMMITMENT CONTRACT

I _____ on this _____ day of _____ 19__ do commit myself to the above described plan that is designed to reduce the level of stress I feel in relation to my **career/career pursuits**. I will evaluate my plan on time. If my plan is not working, I will make adjustments as they are needed, or choose an alternate plan.

Signature_____ Date_____ 19__

Witnessed by: _____ Date_____ 19__

_____ Date_____ 19__

<u>EVALUATION</u>:   Date _____ 19___

1.   Refer to **T-SMS II** (page 107). In the space provided, record the current (to date) level of stress you feel for the category of **career/career pursuits.**

2.   Compare the level of stress recorded in **T-SMS I** to that recorded in **T-SMS II,** and register the information below:

T-SMS I level of stress   _____

T-SMS II level of stress   _____

Decrease or increase in level of
stress.   Subtract _____

3.   Based on the decrease or increase in your level of stress, is your plan working? Yes____   No____

4.   If no, what is interfering with your plan?

a. _____

b. _____

5.   Do you need adjustment in your plan? Yes___ No___

6.   If yes, what adjustments can be made?

a. _____

b. _____

7.   Do you need another plan? Yes____ No ____

8.   If yes, in order of specific steps, what is your alternative plan(s)?

a. _____

b. _____

CHAPTER 10.

Social Interacting

SOCIAL INTERACTING consists of the time we spend interacting with others outside the home. This includes relatives, friends, and associates. It does not include our spouse or lover unless that person is with us during social relations and interactions. Our social relations are our secondary support system. It is an important aspect of our lives, but should not replace or become a way of avoiding our primary support system, the home. A significant social relationship can lighten the need to share our lives, but it should not replace or fulfill the need to share with our most intimate loved ones in the home. As mentioned previously, sharing should be done in its proper place, otherwise it can perpetuate rather than help alleviate problems that cause stress.

GOAL ASSESSMENT:

Using the space provided, answer True or False to the following statements:

1. I have someone to talk to when I   _____
    have problems in my relationship.

2. I seldom have time to spend with my   _____
    friends.
3. Other people I know are concerned   _____

about me and how I feel.

4. I have a close circle of friends
    I see a lot.   _____

5. I can and do discuss my innermost
    worries and feelings with someone.   _____

6. I seldom, if ever, socialize with
    employees outside of work.   _____

7. I wish I had someone to talk to
    when I have serious financial
    problems.   _____

8. I don't get to visit with relatives
    as often as I would like.   _____

9. I take the time to hear others
    problems when they want to talk
    to someone.   _____

10. My friends complain that they
    don't see me often enough.   _____

11. I can and do discuss difficult and
    embarrassing health problems and
    worries with my doctor.   _____

12. I don't have enough time to make
    new friends.   _____

13. It's a waste of energy to share with
    others because no one really listens
    anyway.   _____

14. I don't know my associates well
    enough.   _____

15. I can share my feelings and emotions
    with someone.   _____

16. I seek professional counseling when
    I need it.   _____

17. Interacting with others is important _____
    to me.

18. I am dissatisfied with the amount of _____
    time I spend interacting with others.

19. I don't bother others with my _____
    problems and would prefer that
    others didn't bother me with theirs.

20. I try to establish close _____
    relationships with others.
==

Interpretation of answers:

For people who have satisfactory social support
systems,

The answer for numbers 1, 3, 4, 5, 9, 11, 15, 16,
17, and 20 tend to be True.

The answer for numbers 2, 6, 7, 8, 10, 12, 13, 14,
18, and 19 tends to be False.

In stress reduction, the purpose and importance of
social interacting is to maintain an adequate
support system. Please reread the section on
support systems in Chapter 4 which describes how
they help to reduce stress.

If fifteen or more of your answers correspond to
the above, it would appear that you maintain an
adequate support system to help meet your needs in
time of stress. Having ten or fewer answers that
correspond suggests that you should set goals to
establish or improve your social relationships.

Suggestions for goals in this area are:

1. Invite a fellow employee to have lunch with you.

2. Be inquisitive about the social activities of others. If they are doing something you would enjoy, ask for an invitation.

3. Set aside time to visit a relative.

4. When you find yourself turning on the TV when you have nothing to do, call a friend or relative instead. Rather than looking through the TV guide for programs to watch, go through your personal phone book and choose a friend to call.

5. Collect telephone numbers of friends and/or associates. Then call them and make plans for getting together when it is convenient for both of you.
===

DECISION AND PLANNING:

1. I should set goals for social interacting.

   Yes _____ No _____

2. If yes, my goals are: _____

_____

3. In order, what are the specific steps I will take to reach my goal?

(a) _____

(b) _____

(c) _____

4. The obstacles (personal and otherwise) that stand in the way of obtaining my goals are:

(a) _____

(b) _____

(c) _____

5. I plan to reduce my obstacles by:

(a) _____

(b) _____

(c) _____

6. Here is a list of persons who can help me with my
   goals and how:

   PERSON   HOW

(a) _____   _____

(b) _____   _____

(c) _____   _____

(d) _____   _____

7. I plan to dicuss my social ineracting goals with
the above named persons.

   Yes _____   No. _____

==

PLAN IMPLEMENTATION AND COMMITMENT:

1. The exact date and time I will commit myself to execute my plan is:

   Date _____   Time _____

2. The persons who will be a witness to my commitment are?

   (a) _____

   (b) _____

3. By what date can I reliably evaluate whether my plan is working? Date_____19__

COMMITMENT CONTRACT

I _____ on this _____ day of _____ 19__ do commit myself to the above described plan that is designed to reduce the level of stress I feel in relation to **social interacting.** I will evaluate my plan on time. If my plan is not working, I will make adjustments as they are needed, or choose an alternate plan.

Signature_____ Date_____19____

Witnessed by:_____ Date_____19____

_____ Date_____19____

EVALUATION: Date_____19__

1.   Refer to **T-SMS II**, (page 107). In the space provided, record the current (to date) level of stress you feel for the category of **social interacting**.

2.   Compare the level of stress reorded in **T-SMS I** to that in **T-SMS II**, and register the information below:

      T-SMS I level of stress   _____

      T-SMS II level of stress   _____

      Decrease or increase in level of stress.   Subtract   _____

3. Based on the decrease or increase in your level of stress, is your plan working? Yes__ No__

4. If no, what is interfering with your plan?

    a. _____

    b. _____

5. Do you need adjustment in your plan? Yes__ No__

6. If yes, what adjustments can be made?

    a. _____

    b. _____

7. Do you need another plan? Yes___ No___

8. If yes, in order of specific steps, what is your alternative plan(s)?

    a. _____

    b. _____

CHAPTER 11.

Miscellaneous Time

MISCELLANEOUS TIME is the time we spend enroute to fulfill other aspects of our lives, such as commuting, paying bills, shopping, etc. Often miscellaneous time is seen as more stressful because it is viewed as wasted time. Here stress can be reduced simply by reducing our miscellaneous time or by better organization of how this time is spent.

GOAL ASSESSMENT:

Using the space provided, answer True or False to the following statements:

1. I hate to commute and always wait
   until the last minute to get started. _____
2. I commute farther than most people. _____
3. I have to commute farther, more
   often, or for longer periods of
   time than I like. _____
4. I travel much more than I like. _____
5. All my free time is used in running
   around or commuting. _____
6. Commuting and running around zaps
   my energy. _____
7. Running erands has the lowest
   priority for me in getting things
   done. _____

8. Commuting or running erands is
    a bore.   _____

9. I wish I could cut down on my
    commute time.   _____

10. I have been commuting too far and
    too long.   _____

==

Interpretation of answers:

There are no right or wrong answers to the above
statements. They are designed to help you get in
touch with your feelings about commuting. If you
feel stress in this area, you should set goals to
bring it to a minimum.

Examples for goals are as follows:

1. Rather than drive to work everyday, take the
train or bus once in a while. When you do, plan
how you will spend your time while riding, e.g.,
take a favorite piece of literature you enjoy, or
the novel you've never had the time to read.

2. Plan your errands according to their proximity
so that you don't waste time covering the same
ground.

3. Investigate car pools. This will save you
money and energy. Be selective and find people you
enjoy riding with.
==

DECISION AND PLANNING:

1. I should set **miscellaneous time** goals for myself?

    Yes _____   No _____

2. If yes, my goals are: _____

_____

3. In order, the specific steps I will take to reach my goal are?

(a) _____

(b) _____

(c) _____

4. The obstacles (personal and otherwise) that stand in the way of obtaining my goals are:

(a) _____

(b) _____

(c) _____

5. I plan to reduce these obstacles by:

(a) _____

(b) _____

(c) _____

6. Here is a list of persons who can help me with my goals and how:

PERSON	HOW
(a) _____	_____
(b) _____	_____
(c) _____	_____

7. I plan to dicuss my miscellaneous goals with the above named persons.

Yes _____ No _____

==

PLAN IMPLEMENTATION AND COMMITMENTS:

1. The exact date and time I will commit myself to execute my plan is:

   Date _____ Time _____

2. The persons who will be a witness to my commitment are:

   (a) _____

   (b) _____

3. The date I can reliably evaluate whether my plan is working is:

   _____19__

COMMITMENT CONTRACT

I _____ on this _____ day of _____ 19__ do commit myself to the above described plan that is designed to reduce the level of stress I feel in relation to **miscellaneous time.** If my plan is not working, I will make adjustments as they are needed, or choose an alternate plan.

Signature_____Date_____19__

Witnessed by: _____Date_____19__

_____Date_____19__

EVALUATION: Date _____19__

1. Refer to **T-SMS II** (page 107).   In the space
    provided, record the current (to date) level
    of stress you feel for the category of **miscellan-
    eous time**.

2. Compare the level of stress recorded in **T-SMS I**
    to that recorded in **T-SMS II**, and register
    the following below:

    T-SMS I level of stress   _____

    T-SMS II level of stress   _____

    Decrease or increase in level of
    stress.   Subtract _____

3. Based on the decrease or increase in your level
    of stress, is your plan working? Yes__ No__

4. If no, what is interfering with your plan?

    a. _____

    b. _____

5. Do you need adjustment in your plan? Yes__ No__

6. If yes, what adjustments can be made?

    a. _____

    b. _____

7. Do you need another plan? Yes___ No___

8. If yes, in order of specific steps, what is
    your alternative plan(s)?

    a. _____

    b. _____

CONCLUSION

The **PSM** program completes the final stage of **Personalized Stress Management** development. As you get started in your program, you should remember that it does not have to be followed religiously or for extended periods of time. That is, it should *Program* not be followed in such a way that the program *should* itself becomes stressful. Following through on *itself not* your commitments in approximation of the time *be stressful* frames you set for your goals is often satisfactory, and no doubt, frequent adjustments will be necessary. Flexibility should be an equal part of your determination.

It is unlikely that you will be able to set goals and keep commitments for all aspects of your life at the same time. To do so would probably be somewhat self-defeating. You should review your T-SMS's and determine what areas need your closest and most immediate attention, and set priorities for your goals accordingly.

It is suggested that you begin setting goals in the aspect of PRIVACY. I see this as a most important area, mainly because it focuses on the self, which is the subject of all your stress. How stress effects you depends on your mental and physical condition, how you receive it and how you deal with it on a minute-by-minute, day-by-day, or ongoing

basis. When you are in good mental and physical
condition, you will be much more successful in
achieving stress-reduction goals in all   other
apects of your life.

If there are particular personal goals you would
like to set for yourself (e.g. a personal hobby
you've always wanted to start, or a negative habit
you feel a strong need to extinguish) that is not
accounted for in the category of PRIVACY, you
should feel free to make use of those sections
whereby your assessments determine that you do not
need to set goals. For example, if your goal
assessment for the subcategory of sleep, or the
category of social interacting determine that you
do not need to set goals, simply cross out that
category title and write in the new goal title you
would like to work towards.   Make full use of the
section.   Feel free to use this flexibility in all
categories as you set up your overall PSM program.

As you proceed through the course of the program,
in case you discover at some point that your
condition of stress is such that you do not have
the   strength or security to set or carryout
realistic goals for yourself as prescribed by the
book   alone,   your program goals become   too
complicated or confusing, or you have exhausted all
conceivable alternatives to gaining personal
control of your stress, you should be reminded that
professional help, assistance, or guidance to get
you started or on the right track, is a viable
alternative in all aspects of your PSM program.

stress,
life & distress
are
ongoing

Living is a lifetime job.   It can be seen as an
endless burdensome struggle, dominated by forces
beyond   our control,   or as an ongoing and
challenging growth experience within the realm of
self-mastery and creativity.   A job means work,
work requires energy,   and energy necessitates
stress.   We cannot live without stress, as stress
is an integral part of life itself.   Your life and
how you manage stress is your trade and no one can
master it better than you.   Mastery of a trade is

not something you are born with, rather it is more
a learning process , a matter of understanding,
skill, and creativity, something everyone has the
potential to develop.

Hopefully this book has provided adequate material
and information for your development of **Personalized Stress Management;** and through its course, you
have gained a sense of self-reliance and mastery
that has internalized the feelings of being in
charge and having command of the stress in your
life.

BIBLIOGRAPHY

(1) Bahm, A.: Yoga: For business executives and professional people. New York, Citadel Press, 1965.

(2) Benson, H.: The Relaxation Response. New York, Morrow, 1975, pgs. 162-163.

(3) Bricklin, M.: Natural Healing. Emmaus, Pennsylvania, Rodale Press, 1976.

(4) Carrington, P.: Freedom in Meditation, New York, Anchor Press, 1977.

(5) Cox, Tom: Stress. Baltimore, Maryland, University Park Press, 1978.

(6) Essentials of Life and Health. Del Mar, California, CRM Books, 1972, pp. 231-67.

(7) Freidman, M.I., and Rosenman, R. H.: Type A Behavior and Your Heart. New York, A. A. Knopf, 1974.

(8) Hilgard, E. R., Atkinson, R. L. and Atkinson, R. C.: Introduction to Psychology. New York, Harcourt Brace Jovanovich, Inc, 1979. pp. 30-64, 417-39.

(9) Holmes, T. H. and Rahe, R. H.: The Social Readjustment Rating Scale. J. Psychosomatic Research 11 (1967): 213-218.

(10) Lakein, A.: How to Get Control of Your time and Your Life, New York, Signet, 1973.

(11) McConnel, J. V.: Understanding Human Behavior. New York, Holt, Rinehart and Winston, 1977. pp. 288-306.

(12) Parrino, J.J.: From Panic to Power: The positive use of stress. New York, John Wiley and Sons, 1979.

(13) Pelletier, K. R.: Holistic Medicine. New York, Delacorte Press, 1979.

(14) Rathus, S. A.: Psychology. New York, Holt, Rinehart and Winston, 1981.

(15) Rodale, J. I.: Rodale's System for Mental Power and Natural Health. Rodale Press, 1966.

(16) Rotter, J. B.: External Control and Internal Control. Psychology Today 5 (1971): 37-42, 58-59.

(17) Selye, H: Stress without Distress. Philadelphia, Lippincott, 1974.

(18) Selye, H.: The Stress of Life. New York, McGraw-Hill, 1976.

(19) Vishnudevananda, S.: The Complete Illustrated Book of Yoga. New York, Bell, 1960.

(20) Wolpe, J.: Behavior Therapy Techniques. New York, Pergamon, 1966.

PSM NOTES

PSM NOTES

PSM NOTES

PSM NOTES